Dedicated to my wife Elsie and my children

Orlando, Roman and Scarlet

"As a teenager, lucid dreaming enabled me to erase tragedies experienced or conversely, re-experience and intensify sensational dreams. I remember sharing my lucid dream experiences with my sister who had similar experiences. I never thought lucid dreaming could be an area of scientific interest. This book brought up new insights and opened up a new dimension of thinking. Motivating me to think of possible applications of lucid dreaming in my field of study. It's so impressive how the author has used simple similes and metaphors to facilitate understanding of complex psychodynamics."

Dr. Indika Neluwa-Liyanage, Department of Biochemistry, Faculty of Medical sciences, University of Sri Jayewardenepura, Sri Lanka

"I read the book Dream Physics with a lot of curiosity. The book is an important first-person contribution of the experiences lived by the author during his many Lucid Dreamings. What the author reports is a very accurate diary of the conditions preceding and following his Lucid Dreamings, compared to the ordinary state of consciousness. The value of these experiences in the first person, is fundamental to expand knowledge of our true nature and the essence of our Consciousness."

Dr Patrizio Tressoldi, Science of Consciousness Research Group, Department of General Psychology, University of Padua, Italy

"This book is very interesting. The author explains odd examples of lucid dreaming and introduces "Creative Science" as a way of classifying lucid dream phenomena drawing on Neuroscience, Psychology and Philosophy. Dream lovers and non-dream lovers alike can both drive into his journey."

Niladri Das, Doctoral Student, Department of Philosophy, Jadavpur University Kolkata, India

"Read this book to find out what it means to step inside your own consciousness."

Gianluca Marzola, Doctoral Student, Cognitive Psychology and Philosophy, Department of Philosophy and Communication Studies, University of Bologna, Italy

Dream Physics

By Damian Amamoo

Inception Strategies Pty Ltd
www.dreamphysics.org

Copyright © 2020 by Damian Amamoo
Published by Inception Strategies Pty Ltd
www.dreamphysics.org

All rights reserved. No part of this book may be reproduced in any manner without written permission except for quotations embodied in reviews or citations in scientific papers. For more information please contact us here www.dreamphysics.org/contact

A catalogue record for this work is available from the National Library of Australia

ISBN 978-0-9925460-5-2

Cover Design: Rochelle Abesamis
Interior Design: Ahammed Sabbir
Dream Illustrations: Tirso Llaneta
Proofing: Diana Sitek, Sam Amamoo
Copy Editing: Mickail Mattioli

Thanks to the following people for their companionship during the year that I wrote this book and being a part of the never ending conversation: Glen, Lea, Gaia, Elliott and Sam, James and Jess, Ana, Carolina, Mark and Jocelyn, Kon, Oliver, Paul and Sally, Tim, Stephanie, Rachel, Phil, Phillippa, Kaleo and Melaina, Harry and Angela, Rebecca, Tamara and Snezana, John and Angela.

Contents

1. Introduction   9
Why is "Dream Physics" needed right now?   11
How it's going to benefit every reader   11

2. Science and the problem of bias   13
What happens when I wear odd-colored shoes?   13
Rose-colored glasses   14
What could we be missing?   15

3. The GUT problem   17
What is a Grand Unified Theory?   17
What is everybody talking about?   17
How are we progressing on it?   18
GUT and the Nature of Matter   19
The role of memory   20
The Amygdala and Hippocampus   21
Brain Consciousness   22
Animal, Plant and Rock Consciousness?   22
Time and Consciousness   25
Gravity and Consciousness   26

4. What are the main barriers to GUT success?   27
What are the main problems holding us back and why?   27
Truth   28
Likeable, Repeatable, Shareable?   28
Communication of Findings   29
Explaining Creative Science   31
Creative Science and the Trinity of Evidence   32

5. A Creative Science framework - Part 1 — 34

Creative Science - Lucid Dreams — 34
Creative Science - Flight Safety — 36
Creative Science - Substances and Drugs — 36
Creative Science - Remembering Dreams — 37
Creative Science - Interpenetration — 37
Creative Science - Everett's Multiverse — 38
Creative Science - Probable Realities — 40
Creative Science - Time — 41
Creative Science - Planes of Existence — 42

6. A Creative Science framework - Part 2 — 44

Creative Science - Physical Body Plane — 44
Creative Science - Etheric Body Plane — 44
Creative Science - Astral Body Plane — 45
Creative Science - Inner Screen — 47

7. My Lucid Dream Journal — 48

Electrical — 49
Stairs — 50
The River — 51
Experiments — 52
Reverse Gravity — 53
Precision Flying — 54
Glide Flying Layer — 55
CSF Swimming — 56
Bellows Breath flying — 58
Brain Chemical Fuel Tank — 60
Astral Bike Ride — 61

Astral Car	62
The Wall	63
China Café	64
Levitation	65
Ocean Promenade	66
Back to Class	70
Pre-Flight Brain Reactions	72
Reflections	74
Action Potential	75
Viscosity 1	76
Viscosity 2	77
In Dual	78
The Shoe	80
Long Distance Flight	81
River Redgum	83
Pre-Flight Rocking	85
Lucid Eye Experiments	86
Words In The Sky	87
Back Flying Innovation!	89
Hidden Things	90
Astral Telekinesis 1	91
Astral Telekinesis 2	92
Molecular Experiment 1	93
Molecular Experiment 2	96
Lucid Participation	97
Double Projection	98
Timber Log	101
Mass increase	102
Projection into Matter	103

8. Lucid Checklist — 105

Trauma — 105
Calm Tips — 105
Getting Comfortable — 106
Heart Listening — 107
Affinity Networks — 108
Rise — 108
Critical Facility — 109

9. The hard problem of consciousness — 110

A conflict of sorts — 110
Our Next Book — 111

10.0 Glossary — 112

References — 118

1. Introduction

> "The future needs people who believe in the beauty of their dreams." Eleanor Roosevelt, Activist

It's 1979 in Adelaide, Australia and I have again woken up in the middle of the night, paralyzed with fear after being chased in my dreams by a spooky thing!

I sit up in bed, grateful to be released from another nightmare, and then pad out to our playroom blanketed in 70's pooh-colored shag carpet. I sit myself down on a matching brown corduroy bean bag and turn on the TV to watch a black and white Gene Autry Western.

I don't know why they played Gene Autry at three o'clock in the morning, but if you asked me at the time, I would have described them as a *lifesaver* for this nine-year old, wiry-legged, afro-haired, chocolate-skinned boy-dreamer.

As I grew older, I became more used to my dream experiences that gradually grew less scary and more inspirational.

Upon leaving home at the age of 22, I began to keep a dream diary of my nightly experiences.

Unfortunately, this early diary with infrequent entries is now lost. But the pain of losing it jolted me into a more rigorous diarization of my dreams that began again when I was in my early 30's and continues up to the present day, giving me nearly 20 years of recorded dream experiences to draw from.

"Dream Physics" began as an idea in my mind when I realized that I had documented a significant number of lucid flying dreams and had paid particular attention to reporting the *physics* of my dream flight experiences.

- Why was it easier to fly upwards than downwards?
- Why did the impact of gravity vary, depending on height?
- Why did some of the dream atmospheres seem highly viscous and involve a lot more friction?
- What were the currents that would sometimes pull me in a certain direction and make straight flying more difficult?
- Why did I get a sensation that certain brain chemicals were necessary to provide "fuel" for flight that was nearly always limited in terms of how long I could fly?

This book provides personal recorded data from direct experience. It will help scientists, quantum physicists, neuroscientists, experimental psychologists, therapists, philosophers and above all you, who realize that dreaming is a valid form of conscious experience that deserves to be taken seriously.

"Dream Physics" can help you become a better dreamer because we are going to teach you about the different environments that we have experienced.

I'm going to cover some theory and frameworks that will enable you to better understand some of the odd, and yet true, lucid-dreaming experiences which I'll introduce in the latter part of the book.

We are going to give scientists new tools for thinking about matter, consciousness and physics. We are going to give you new inner tools to explore your lucid truth and draw greater pleasure from your waking and sleeping experiences.

The conscious activity of reading the book should by itself set you along a path of change. On behalf of the "Dream Physics" team we sincerely welcome you to our world.

Why is "Dream Physics" needed right now?

"Dream Physics" is needed right now because humanity is on an unsustainable trajectory. Yes, we have technological brilliance but we also have people who are killing each-other over religious differences. We have scientists struggling to reconcile the quantum world and our macro-physical world. We have billions suffering from depression and valuing their lives only in terms of what they are able to physically create for themselves. We have a global environment that is literally melting, on fire, hyper-barren, flooding or riven by pandemics. We have animal and plant kingdoms under extreme pressure with growing extinctions. And we have swirling misinformation & distortions that make it difficult for many people to experience truth.

Solving this is going to require people and a solution that is human-led. Sustainable solutions for our species and planet will require new breeds of science that are able to push into areas that it's presently struggling to reach.

"Dream Physics" is a drop in the ocean of the change that is required, but it is also about the ocean in the drop. This book will draw attention to a lucid doorway that is available to each of one us to explore the unknown and talk about our findings. "Dream Physics" would like *everyone, everywhere* to start talking about their dreams and their personal journey to find their own truth.

How it's going to benefit every reader

"Dream Physics" is not the answer to whether you should stay in a house, buy a car, get married or take a new job. It's not about dream-catchers, séances, mysticism, voodoo or magic. It's not about any one religion over another. It's not going to help you find a soul mate, a new pet or a workout regime.

"Dream Physics" is about developing a new lens we are going to call "Creative Science". We will show you how each one of us can practice Creative Science by recording our dream experiences and looking for recurring and repeating patterns.

"Dream Physics" is going to break science down to its fundamentals - out of the research facilities and back into the hands of each one of us with eyes, ears, a brain and the ability to write. This needs to happen because paid science (i.e. the science industry) needs our help. They are running up against theoretical walls, mathematical barriers, measurement problems, dark matter they cannot see and quantum entanglements that are difficult to make sense of. Paid scientists are pushing deeper into the heart of matter and the further they go, the more they are finding that no-thing seems to be there. They are breaking down their instruments, building longer and faster colliders and refining new mathematics in a desperate race to discover the origin point of matter.

"Dream Physics" will be a wake-up call for progressive scientists who will have a "down tools" moment as they read this book and come away from the experience with new lenses to tackle the problems they are working on. "Dream Physics" is going to take a birds-eye view of science as it stands, about the fundamental challenges and opportunities. We are going to have a look at some of the thinking that is holding us back and suggest some alternative ways forward.

Then, we are going to sketch out a theoretical framework that will help you get the most from your lucid dream experiences and talk about your dream life with friends, family and even colleagues.

Lastly, we will detail the lucid-flying and other dreams I have directly experienced with commentary. Dreams, that are all part of my own lucid truth. We're not pretending this is going to be easy. You might have some moments where you feel like walking away because it seems *odd*, or it doesn't fit with your worldview. Or maybe because your head hurts thinking about the ramifications, or because you simply don't believe it's possible that anyone can experience lucid-dreams. But stay with us and you will benefit. There is simply no other outcome.

You will find something in this book that resonates with you. Whether you are a scientist or not. A dreamer or not. Or just someone with a sense of adventure.

2. Science and the problem of bias

> "Choose your habits as if your life depends on them, because it does." Gift Gugu Mona, Philosopher

What happens when I wear odd-colored shoes?

You will have noticed by now the odd-colored shoes on the cover of this book. I bought the shoes some years ago as two reasonably identical pairs, one blue and the other maroon. Sometimes, when I am of a certain mind, I wear them out for the day and am always fascinated by the reactions I get. Some people look at me like I am an oddball, others have a look of curious confusion, as though they are trying to work out whether I am making a fashion statement. Some seem perfectly comfortable with it and still others give me such a look, that you would think that I was instead walking upside down on my head!

There's nothing spectacular about wearing odd-colored shoes. It's something that any of us can do. So why don't we? Because shoes are sold in identical pairs? Because most people only buy one pair of shoes at a time?

Both of these statements are true but they still don't fully address why we don't have more examples of people wearing different colored shoes? After all, we have different color shirts, jackets and even hair, so why not shoes? Does it have something strange to do with the fact that shoes are on the ground and therefore need to be of the same color?

Why do we even call odd shoes "odd"?

> "In matters of style, swim with the current; in matters of principle, stand like a rock." Thomas Jefferson

Perhaps this is not the earth-shattering problem that it threatens to be? Provided that the universe is not hiding any odd shoes? Indulging ourselves further, we can even imagine a scale of "oddness."

MILDLY ODD EVENTS	INCREDIBLY ODD EVENTS

Beginning with events that are only mildly odd on the left, for example, through to behavior on the right that seems incredibly odd. Our little oddness scale underlies expectations that new discoveries should, in at least some ways, conform to the same pattern as the old ones. If they don't, people can say regardless of a mathematical proof, that they simply don't *like* a hypothesis and find it difficult to support. A researcher can find his or her odd hypothesis rejected by a supervisor. Or equally, a completed but odd paper might not be accepted by a journal selection committee for publishing and therefore vanishes into obscurity (Scientific American 2008).

Rose-colored glasses

> "One has the feeling that it is precisely the most important statement of the new theory that can be squeezed into these Spanish boots - but only with difficulty," Albert Einstein in a letter to Charles Schrodinger about entanglement (Crull 2019).

Would it be wrong to say for modern science to discover new truths that:

- The event must be physically observable
- The new truth should in some ways conform to existing truths
- The method of data collection must be reliable
- The hypotheses must be liked by the scientific establishment and not seen as odd? (Funk 2018)

If we turn our thoughts to the search for a unified theory of everything that is wrestled with by our quantum physicists, we find that the most popular theory known as the *Copenhagen Interpretation* borrows and builds upon much older classical theory that was established by Newton and others.

The Copenhagen Interpretation claims that the inconsistencies involved with what happens between the quantum world and our normal macro-world is okay and nothing to worry about because they are separate worlds and should be treated as such. This view is currently liked by our scientific establishment and not seen as odd.

Notwithstanding there are other physicists who believe there are inconsistencies involved with the idea of separate treatment for our quantum and macro-worlds and that we should be looking for a theory that makes them part of the one system.

What could we be missing?

> "I don't like that man. I must get to know him better." Abraham Lincoln

Despite the differences in perspectives, if we have established that likeability or distance from oddness is a real bias in paid science, then have we not hand-cuffed ourselves into searching only for that which is physically observable, testable, mathematically verifiable, repeatable, popular and conforming?

As limiting as this might sound to some, for others it could be business as usual and if we are not in the midst of a scientific crisis or a state of quantum emergency then why rock the boat? Logic would say that scientists who have the most to gain by working to retain the status quo will do so. Other scientists who have the most to gain by introducing new breakthroughs will ceaselessly niggle at the existing scientific criteria to give up any inherent weaknesses and flaws.

Speaking of flaws, it is necessary for us at this time to insert a seed of an idea for you to consider. It goes something like this:

> "Is it possible, among the estimated 93 billion light years of space out there in the universe, that there could be hiding, at least one *odd shoe event* that by itself exists, but for our purposes is only partially observable, hardly measurable and definitely not conforming to what we have discovered so far?"

3. The GUT problem

> "What you do makes a difference, and you have to decide what kind of difference you want to make." Dr. Jane Goodall

What is a Grand Unified Theory?

> "We perceive the operation of a force which is mixed up with everything that exists in the heavens or on earth; which pervades every atom, rules the motions of animate and inanimate beings, and is as sensible in the descent of a rain-drop as in the falls of Niagara; in the weight of the air, as in the periods of the moon." (Somerville 1846)

Nothing to do with stomachs, the idea of a GUT or Grand Unified Theory of everything that ties together light, gravity, nuclear and electromagnetic forces, consciousness, space and matter into a single theory has inspired movies, books, scientific treatises, hypotheses and so on.

What is everybody talking about?

They are wanting, seeking, searching for a way to merge all these forces into a single coherent and explainable force (Francis 2016). No small undertaking in our complex world with a myriad diversity of events happening. One could be forgiven for thinking it fanciful and absurd to even attempt to tie it all together. Nonetheless, the quest for a GUT marches on.

Perhaps it has more to do with the human side of ourselves that yearns for interconnectedness and meaning? Maybe in searching for a GUT, humanity is trying to project an idea of "one-ness" into a system where it simply doesn't exist.

Maybe we should be listening to the Copenhagen Interpretationists after all and be satisfied that our universe is divided up into parcels that don't need to share the same physics?

How are we progressing on it?

Our quest for GUT is surging ahead on two major fronts - quantum physics and neuroscience theories of consciousness.

Quantum physics is wrestling with the measurement problem that says a quantum event with two possible outcomes, can be interfered with by a person who simply steps in to measure the event. The simple act of measuring actually changes the probability of the event outcome. The upshot suggests we are all living in a *participatory universe* where the actions of different events are directly related to our conscious decisions.

But the "oddness" doesn't stop there. Quantum physicists have shown that two different particles can maintain a relationship with each other even if they are separated by massive distances of several light years and are at the opposite ends of the universe. Such particles are said to be entangled with each other and while the mathematics of the relationship holds, some scientists are finding it a little uncomfortable and odd.

> "I know of course how the hocus pocus works mathematically, but I do not like such a theory." Charles Schrodinger talking about Quantum Entanglement in a letter to Einstein (Crull 2019)

As much as we may not like it, undiscovered reality may not be inclined to fit in with all of our scientific expectations. As thinkers we need to be crystal clear about who needs to be flexible?

Is it reasonable for us as scientists to expect the diversity of the universe to fit inside our thinking? Or could we be better served, by resting our models for a moment and developing some lucid-dream-based observation techniques that will provide new data and crucial insights into the greater diversity of ourselves and the universe?

GUT and the Nature of Matter

> "Every block of stone has a statue inside it and it is the task of the sculptor to discover it." Michelangelo

GUT is seeking to solve the question of what is beneath matter?

When we stick our mathematical microscope down into the quantum world to take a look we might be lucky enough to see an electron. Our momentary surge of excitement is then cut short as our spinning electron strangely disappears in front of our eyes and then reappears somewhere else a few seconds later?

The prickly discomfort this is causing our scientists is, " Where on God's earth did it go?"

There are theories abounding that such electrons disappear into another world that exists beneath physical matter. One point of view is that our electron changed state into a one-dimensional "string" and became part of a network of strings that connect with each-other throughout the universe (Siegel 2016).

Another popular theory says, our little electron disappeared to become part of a "dark energy" or "dark-matter" universe that exists, but is not possible for us to measure at the current time. (Tate 2013)

An alternative concept is that our electron disappeared to become part of the "consciousness as energy" universe. Leading us along to a startling idea that consciousness could be an origin point or state of matter. (The Physics arXiv Blog 2014)

No matter whether you think such an idea is wildly dubious or whether you are intuitively attracted to it, it is promoting an investigation into an expanded theory of consciousness. (Heaven 2015)

It almost sounds like the beginnings of a unified theory or GUT, but before we get ahead of ourselves, let's take a closer look at the problem of trying to understand consciousness.

Insofar as neuroscience theories are concerned, most research effort is going into understanding the brain and its contribution to consciousness. Let's begin by having a look at memory.

The role of memory

Memory is a characteristic of consciousness. In other words, if consciousness was a color, for example, purple, then memory could be described as one of the input colors (i.e. red or blue), that help make our conscious experience what it is. For example, a person with dementia might undergo a memory "reset" every few days, so they are unable to remember anything before that point, and can only recollect very recent experiences. Such people are still living, breathing and conscious, yet their experience of consciousness is different to what we are normally accustomed to.

Have the older memories of a person with dementia disappeared? Or are they back there somewhere, still existing as perfect records? Yet irretrievable, because the person's present neural and psychological machinery is unable to provide the same level of support?

Such questions can run us straight into the mind-body problem and have us wondering whether our experiences are stored directly in the brain or whether some other storage facilities are also being used?

For example, are there other organs in the body, that have some yet-to-be-discovered role to play in the working of human memory? Or are there consciousness "structures" situated off-site from the body that also have a function?

Questions that are not easy to answer.

Let's dive into brain science and look at two very important memory structures in the brain that impact on consciousness; the Amygdala and the Hippocampus.

The Amygdala and Hippocampus

The amygdala sits alongside the hippocampus in our brain and is responsible for how we record emotions to memory. Science suggests that the amygdala is part of the brain's first response "engine" that sees and reacts to our environment. Like a supercharged concert composer, the amygdala assesses the environment emotionally and then links through to other parts of our brain so fast that it alters our memory and perception of events as they occur (McGaugh, Cahill, Roozendahl 1996).

We can simplify the relationship between the amygdala and hippocampus by visualizing them as brother and sister organs. The hippocampus remembers *what* happens and the amygdala remembers the *emotion* attached to the event.

For example, if a child is stung by a bee, it is the amygdala that records the emotional pain of the bee sting, whilst the hippocampus records the scene, the bee and the process of events. If we had a magic wand and took the child's amygdala offline and re-introduced the bee we would find the child remembers that the bee causes a sting, but the child would show no fear about the outcome.

Conversely, if we shook our magic wand and this time brought the child's amygdala back online and took their hippocampus offline and reintroduced the bee, we would likely find the child afraid at seeing the bee but would not be able to remember why they are afraid of it (Phelps 2006).

What are the different theories of consciousness that such memories can be a part of?

Brain Consciousness

One brain-based theory says that consciousness is an informational process that "arrives" or "appears" from a constant stream of human thought. An appealing concept that implies more questions, such as how many thoughts are required to make that stream? How fast do these thoughts need to travel? Do they all need to be of a certain structure and so on?

Brain hemispheres are continually being mapped for functions and there is a lot of work going into brain-compatible circuitry and human/brain interfaces. Interfaces that are likely to challenge our present understanding of consciousness as we attempt to explain the symbiosis between humanity and machines.

Another growing but contested theory of consciousness is Integrated Information Theory that has the backing of some prominent neuroscientists yet, surprisingly, skates down a panpsychist perspective saying that: "every physical object has some (even if extremely low) level of consciousness" (Barratt 2018).

Such a view causes problems for most people who have grown up in a world that only counts people as being conscious.

Animal, Plant and Rock Consciousness?

The idea of animals being capable of having consciousness is yet to be widely accepted by the scientific community. Nonetheless, in 2012, a prominent international group of cognitive neuroscientists, neuropharmacologists, neuroanatomists, neurophysiologists and computational neuroscientists joined together and made the following:

Cambridge Declaration on Consciousness

> "The weight of evidence indicates that humans are not unique in possessing the neurological substrates that generate consciousness. Nonhuman animals, including all mammals and birds, and many other creatures, including octopuses, also possess these neurological substrates (Low, Panksepp, Reiss, Edelman, Swinderen & Koch 2012)."

If we are to entertain such notions, how far does it go? What about plant consciousness? Where is science standing on that?

A group of seven like-minded researchers led by Lincoln Taiz from the University of South Carolina made the following declaration in a published paper for the journal *Trends in Plant Science:*

> "There is no evidence that plants require, and thus have evolved, energy-expensive mental faculties, such as consciousness, feelings, and intentionality, to survive or to reproduce (Taiz, Alkon, Draguhn, Murphy, Blatt, Hawes, Thiel, Robinson 2019)."

Despite such statements about plant consciousness, there are other scientists who disagree with them, most notably the Australian scientist, Dr. Monica Gagliano and author of "Thus Spoke the Plant," who says:

> "If we think we already know how things are and fail to continuously question our own assumptions, but construct our claims on a system of beliefs we are dearly attached to, then we are in deep trouble and miss the opportunity for true scientific discovery to occur (Sample 2019)."

Likewise, Plant researcher and Nobel Prize Winner, Barbara McClintock once said:

> "Every time I walk on grass, I feel sorry because I know the grass is screaming at me" (Keller 1984).

What about inanimate matter such as rocks and the like? Could they be conscious?

Philosophy of the Mind professor at New York University, David Chalmers, who famously laid out the hard problem of consciousness in 1995, says that there are interpretations of panpsychism that

> "Rocks will be conscious, spoons will be conscious, the Earth will be conscious, any kind of aggregation gives you consciousness" (Godhill 2018).

Such concepts make one wonder, if true, how does the experience of consciousness change as we progress from rocks to plants to animals to people? Do rocks have memories? Can plants communicate? Can animals dream?

Let's pull the rip-cord on our panpsychist adventure for the time being and explore another important aspect of consciousness - time.

Time and Consciousness

As humans, we tend to organize our conscious experience into a linear sequence of events that helps us to remember, compare, and share our lives with others. Time is the fundamental reference point that allows us to participate in consecutive conscious experiences that carry meaning. Dinner is after lunch, that is after breakfast that was after bedtime the day before, and so on. Time presses against us and seemingly cannot be beaten.

If it was possible to adjust time, let's say via the movement of a dial on a very fancy-looking black box and we decided to turn the dial to "freeze time", then would everyone around us simply freeze in their tracks? If we walked around the room to look at each person, would they be at risk because they are not able to take a breath to support their body and stay alive? Or would they not need to breathe because every part of their body, down to the cells and molecules would exist in a temporary stasis, living and yet not living, until we again adjusted the dial on the box?

Is time really the constant, metronomic force of precision that we imagine it to be? If for example, an entangled particle at one end of the universe can update its phase faster than the speed of light in response to a change in the phase of its "sister" particle on earth. Then we may have some fun with this and consider that there may be more flavors of time than lemon and lime? Or in other words, there may be different experiences of time depending on the perspective from which time is viewed or observed.

Is time unassailable? Or does it bend and change shape to match the environment or patch of universe it is working through?

Brad Skow, an associate professor of philosophy at MIT, introduced a new theory of time called the *block universe* that builds on Einstein's conception of space-time. In his book Objective Becoming, Skow says that the past and future continue to exist as much as the present and our life is like a spotlight moving across an ever present dimension of space-time (Dizikes 2015), (Navilon 2019).

Let's dispense with time for now and investigate a more rock-solid concept- gravity, which is a favourite of our scientists because it conforms to established classical laws, is predictable and mathematically verifiable.

Gravity and Consciousness

Does gravity have a role to play in consciousness?

If we were placed into a spaceship in orbit around the earth and there was no gravity inside the ship, does our experience of consciousness change? We feel lighter and the load on our muscles seems to be different. If we push away from a wall and float towards the opposite wall, there is a changed feeling of inertia and resistance to slowing down. We may have a different sensation of our own body weight and our breathing may also feel different, so does our consciousness change as well?

If we look out the window of the spaceship and see a comet made of radioactive material, science tells us that depending on the elements present, the rock should be in an ongoing state of decay and gradually losing mass. If we could throw our consciousness into the rock as it flew past, would we experience a change in the consciousness of the rock as it became influenced by the gravitational pull of the planets it passes? Could such a rock have some way of storing its own conscious experience? Is there an aspect of memory recording, storage or retrieval that is affected by gravity? Or is there no relationship?

With so many hard questions unanswered we may be forgiven for temporarily abandoning our quest for a Grand Unified Theory. Why are we having such a difficult time of it?

4. What are the main barriers to GUT success?

> "A man who has committed a mistake and doesn't correct it, is committing another mistake" Confucius, Chinese Philosopher and reformer 551 BC - 479 BC

> "Physics is puzzle solving, too, but of puzzles created by nature, not by the mind of man." Maria Goeppert-Mayer, Physics Nobel Prize Winner

What are the main problems holding us back and why?

The following three problems could weaken our quest for a GUT:

- Truth or the way the universe really is - whether we can discover it or not?
- The need for likeable, repeatable experiments that are readily shareable with others.
- The communication of findings to the broader community.

Truth

The first problem is the truth about how the universe really is.

The truth does not care about Nobel prizes, whether you can walk on two legs, whether you can build a spaceship or whether you are more inclined to dreaming about the stars. It doesn't care if you have money, a reputation to uphold, scientific standing, university qualifications, a massive underground Hadron collider or a little stick to make some nice patterns in the sand.

The truth doesn't care about oddness, popularity, conformity, being simple to understand or even being mathematically verifiable. It doesn't care whether you are alive or dead, or somewhere in between, whether you own a dog or whether you have a big research grant. The truth doesn't care about gravity, time, space or distance. It doesn't care about other forms of life that may or may not exist in the universe. As far as the truth is concerned, they either do exist or they don't.

The truth just is. Science needs to discover the truth. It's not truth's job to reveal itself to science.

Nonetheless, there may be data out there that begs to be discovered, providing we, as humans, can become more flexible about finding it.

Likeable, Repeatable, Shareable?

The second problem is the need for likeable, repeatable experiments that are readily shareable with others. We have seen that if a hypothesis is odd or non-conforming, that it may not be funded by a scientific research project? If it is very odd, there may not be any established scientists willing to take the reputational risk of working on it at all.

What if the actual observation, in its minutiae of detail, is virtually impossible to repeat? What if the relevant tools available to conduct the investigation are not easy to share during the event point?

All of these issues are relevant if we are talking about lucid dream data.

Communication of Findings

The third problem lies in the communication of findings to the broader community. This is because the existing system of scientific credit can stymie new researchers, who may be offering a novel approach to a longstanding problem, but find their ideas blocked or abandoned.

Alternately, novel researchers can have their findings token-modified so that somebody else takes the credit. For example, do we really believe that for the one hundred and twelve times the Nobel Prize in Physics has been awarded since 1901, that there have been no more than three women who deserve enough credit to take home a prize? (Nobel 2019)

Doesn't that sound a little odd?

Nonetheless, we shouldn't blame professional scientists about the problems with science or the lack of progress in the search for a GUT. Scientists have families too and need to pay bills like everybody else. As much as some scientists might like to try and test an odd hypothesis, invariably they would have to obtain approval from their supervisor who might laugh in their faces, or worse.

Despite its cautionary culture, contemporary science has been able to take us a long way with its established investigative tools. Scientists do deserve credit for what they have been able to achieve and their discoveries are helping us to inch closer towards a GUT. Yet, these gains are unfortunately not enough and now we find that science has reached a theoretical and practical precipice.

It is as if all of humankind is on one side of a mountain looking across to the other side that represents the data that we need to complete our Grand Unified Theory. But in between is a yawning chasm of the "the world beneath matter," and no rope-bridge to walk across. Try as we might with physical tools, science will eventually realize, that in order to manipulate in the non-physical worlds that lie beneath matter, one requires non-physical tools that are made of the same material that is native to those systems. These tools and materials are available to every human being via meditation and lucid dreaming.

Despite such ideas, there will be dye in the wool scientists who refuse to leave their physical tools or consider any data that is collected without them. But equally there will be other scientists who are experiencing frustration, as one experiment after another yields some information, but not enough.

We believe that human thinking is now at a critical turning point that will usher in a rational, scientific exploration of inner reality. These *Creative Scientists* will be motivated to action by the idea that for highly challenging datasets, such as the world beneath matter, simply getting the required data can sometimes be more important than how you get the data.

Serious scientists will put down tools and start learning how to meditate, lucid dream and build on some of the ideas and lucid dream events in this book. The data they gain from their own lucid-dreaming will help to inform their research priorities and then these creative scientists will pluck scientific progress seemingly from nowhere and the rest of the scientific establishment will be wondering how they did it.

> "I immediately loved working with flies. They fascinated me, and followed me around in my dreams." Christiane Nüsslein-Volhard, Geneticist and Medicine Nobel Prize winner.

Despite these changes, there will be scientists who cling to the idea that our universe is a matter-only universe. But such scientists should ask themselves the following:

If we live on a diverse planet with approximately 8.7 million species of life, in a diverse galaxy with 30 billion other planets and there are estimated to be over 100 billion other galaxies in the observable physical universe. Then would it not be odd, to have not even one, non-matter system in the universe. At one end of a matter-systems-spectrum. That has super dense black holes at the other end? (Science Daily 2011), (Cambridge Astronomy 2012).

Explaining Creative Science

Creative Science is about science for everyone. It's about realizing that if we are to reach the odd observations so badly required then a number of things are going to have to change. For example, we are so used to scientific observations being captured using machines that it's got to the point that if data hasn't been "machine-acquired" then it's not treated as real data.

If we as individuals have an insightful experience of our own, we doubt its validity. We don't know what to do with the information or where to guide it in such a way that it might be helpful to someone doing research. We are worried about what people might think of us or what they might say, so we keep it to ourselves.

> "I was in bed and I saw my body float out through a closed window. I then hovered about our house and the feeling was exhilarating. As I hovered I noticed a pattern of sticks and leaves on the flat roof of our house. Gradually I started to soar backwards and forwards about 30 meters above the house and then along the street. As I swung backwards and forwards, the feeling of exhilaration changed to one of being out of control and I willed myself to stop the gyrations. The next thing I registered was that I was back in bed. So strong was the feeling that the next day I got the ladder and climbed up onto the roof and was shocked to see that the pattern of sticks and leaves was as I had 'seen' it in my out-of-body experience. This shook me up so much that I did not mention anything about what I had experienced for the next 30 years."

When a senior Australian government official had this lucid dream, he was concerned about how people might view him professionally if he spoke of it and so he kept quiet about it for 30 years until after his career was over.

If we multiply this experience by the billions of other people around the world who dream and don't record it or talk about it. We are potentially looking at billions of lucid dreams being lost from our society. Because we haven't in our age of technological brilliance, been able to find a way to make lucid dreams and Creative Science an everyday topic.

This dream data deficit is not just a lost opportunity for scientific progress, it also is a mark against our civilization and culture in the age of the twenty first century. Creative Science would say that lucid dream observations are scientifically valid because they are data. The more data we are able to capture as lucid dreamers, the more we can begin to see patterns emerge. And if we have the confidence to share these patterns, we might find that other people are experiencing them too. If researchers find a way to group these patterns together, they may find odd new hypotheses emerging that warrant further investigation. By sharing our Creative Science experiences, we can all play our part in humanity's reaching towards a GUT.

Creative Science and the Trinity of Evidence

What would Creative Science have to say about our evidentiary trinity that data needs to be:

- Physically observable?
- Testable by others and mathematically verifiable?
- Repeatable?

Physically observable suggests that the observation needs to be made by an alert, awake individual with eyes open and not someone who is sleeping with their eyes closed having a lucid dream. Creative Science would allow that a person is able to use their sight in a lucid dream context, providing that such observations were later recorded in a written or audio format that was accessible to others.

Testable and mathematically verifiable suggests whatever observation has been made, that a control can be set up for appropriate scientific comparison. This might work fine for physical experiments but not so well for unpredictable, once-in-a-lifetime, lucid dream experiences that may offer extraordinary glimpses into scientifically relevant environments. We are also going to have some challenges applying mathematics to lucid, out-of-body experiences that can't be measured in the dream using physical tools. Creative Science would recognize that lucid dream experiences can be highly personalized and very difficult to recreate in an exact sense, yet it would not dismiss the data. Creative Science would search for patterns in the structure of a dream, the way it unfolded, the behavior of characters, the manipulation of objects, environmental physics and the experience of feelings.

Repeatable suggests that an experiment could be repeated anywhere in the world and produce the same results. While some lucid dream experiences, such as flying, may be attainable by a great number of people, the actual characteristics of dream-flight experiences can vary requiring innovative ways of scientifically classifying the data. Creative Science would ask questions such as: "When did you fly? How did you fly? How did it feel? Was it easier to go up or down? Did you have a sense of speed, distance, friction, gravity, inertia, mass et cetera?"

In the next section we will introduce a Creative Science Framework for Lucid Dreaming.

5. A Creative Science framework - Part 1

> "You are unique, and if that is not fulfilled then something has been lost." Martha Graham, Choreographer

If we are to make sense of the odd and unexplainable, we must ourselves become odd. We must look into spaces where it seems that no thing exists. We must develop odd new types of mathematics and physics. We need to clothe and immerse ourselves odd approaches to new and old hypotheses. We need to become the odd that we seek lest we never see what will be in the final moment right under our noses.

Rather than jump straight into highlights of nearly 20 years of lucid dreams. We are going to first outline a framework for Creative Science that we have cobbled together to explain the wide variability of lucid dreaming experiences that are possible.

Creative Science - Lucid Dreams

Most definitions of lucid-dreaming talk about being awake when you are dreaming. The use of the word "awake" is problematic, as "awake" means physically awake and no longer sleeping.

Most people think of lucid dreaming as requiring two elements; one - active participation in dream decisions, and two - remembering a high degree of dream detail. Many lucid dreamers seem to be motivated by opportunities to "control" dreams.

Personally, I am more skewed towards the remembering part of lucid dreaming in my own work, as it's no use being the best lucid dream "director" shaping dream events if you can't remember the dream afterwards. Someone who is less skilled at dream "direction" but highly skilled at remembering the fine detail of dreams is a valuable lucid dreamer because detailed scientific remembering requires high lucidity.

The dreamer may or may not be choosing to exercise all the choices or control available to them in the dream because they are subsumed with the science of recording the data. Such dreamers are still lucid dreaming and capable of making worthwhile contributions to dream science.

Experienced lucid dreamers are likely to understand that lucid dreams will only "put up" with being controlled to a certain degree and that the art of dream direction is being able to maintain a balance between making choices and going with the flow.

We prefer to define lucid-dreaming as:

> "Training the conscious mind to participate in the dreaming process by making decisions and remembering the minutiae of dream details for later recording."

Another way of thinking about this is imagining a slider on a timeline that reflects your lucidity at any point in time during your sleep. One end of the timeline, would have you fully awake and no longer dreaming and the other end will have you dreaming but not lucid. Lucid dreaming is what happens between the two ends when there is an active blend between these two extremes.

The word training recognizes that there is an ongoing bidding war for the precious resources of your conscious ego that is constantly trying to divide itself between work, love, family, projects and life. Fitting in something like lucid-dreaming doesn't happen automatically. We need to find a way to signal to our conscious ego that lucid-dreaming is important and the best way to do this is by performing some type of conscious activity related to dreaming. Like writing in a dream diary, talking about your dreams, illustrating your dreams, thinking about your dreams or even singing about them!

If you can follow through with this over a sustained period of time, your conscious ego should eventually sliver off some of its precious resources to help you better remember and participate in your lucid dreams.

Creative Science - Flight Safety

The most common fear we encounter when discussing lucid dreaming is that people are concerned they might leave their body and somehow not be able to get back into it. In our experience, this is practically impossible. During lucid dreaming we are connected to our physical body at all times. Even though we might be visiting "another world", we are most often doing so without leaving our bedroom.

Some lucid dreamers talk about a silver cord connecting the travelling consciousness with the physical body. I personally have never seen such a cord, but no matter where I have found myself lucid dreaming, I've never experienced a problem returning to my physical body in an instant. Therefore the integrity of the body is never breached or broken by lucid-dreaming.

Creative Science - Substances and Drugs

There are people who talk about using drugs to incite out-of-body experiences or to improve their lucid dreams. There is also research being undertaken to identify the similarities between some drug-induced states and lucid-dreaming (Sanz, Zamberlan, Erowid, Erowid, Tagliazucchi 2018).

I did experiment a little in my university days with some drugs, however, I found that they did not improve my lucid-dreaming or out-of-body experiences. Mostly, they made them worse. Drugs can launch you into unusual planes and environments without any semblance of personal control, which is essential to navigate and coordinate yourself in a meaningful way.

If your goal is to be swept away by an inner tsunami, then drugs can do this for you, but they can also damage the psyche and place you no further down the road to your own spiritual progress. Once you accept there are no shortcuts to this opportunity you will be making progress and should find that a lucid super-dream that appears after months of gradual effort is worth more than a hundred drug-enabled hallucinations.

Creative Science - Remembering Dreams

Remembering dreams is not necessarily an easy thing to do and is an ability I have built up over a long period of time. In the early days, I used to wake up directly after the dream, switch the light on and write in my dream diary, to the acute annoyance of my wife. Happily, this practice eventually gave way to "morning remembering" so that I could wake up and recall dream after dream.

These days, I am using a different technique where I can fully wake myself up directly after a dream, and then go through a mental and emotional process where I fix the minutiae of the dream to memory, before I resume sleep. This exercise can take up to 15 minutes per dream but results in a better level of recall in the morning when I come to record them. Further, the mental-fixing process is especially handy for those lucid dreams that occur early in the evening, as they can be the hardest to recall in the morning light.

If you find yourself waking up in the morning without any recollection of your dreams, try not to worry or feel emotional about it. Place your desire to remember your dreams to the side and allow your day to unfold naturally. You may be surprised to find that something during the day triggers the memory of the dream that was there all along; like a little gemstone under the leaves, waiting for the right breath of wind to uncover and lay it bare for you to re-experience.

Creative Science - Interpenetration

Interpenetration is one of the most important Creative Science concepts for our lucid dreaming framework.

If we place a large cat inside a shoebox there may not be much room for a second cat. We can make some air holes in the box for the first cat, so it is comfortable, but this doesn't change the capacity or volume of the box to be able to host a second cat. Most of us will have trouble visualizing the insertion of a second cat into the shoebox while the first large cat is still there. You'll say that there simply is not enough space for a second cat. It's only a shoebox after all. Everybody knows it's not possible for two different physical items to take up the same portion of space simultaneously.

It's either one or the other.

Now I would like you to imagine that we found a brilliant mathematical equation that we could apply to cat number two. This formula will find a way to "compress" cat two, not so the cat is any smaller, but compressed so that the second cat can coexist and interpenetrate the same space as the first cat in the box, without difficulty and without interference. If we looked inside the box from our earth physical body, we would only see cat one. If we use the mathematics equation to change our own body into the same compression instance as cat two, then we would only see cat two in the box and cat one would be invisible to us. If we could somehow see "in dual" from both perspectives at the same time, we could correctly assert that there are actually two cats in the shoebox, somehow simultaneously taking up the same space.

Both cats are physical cats and if we could interview them (and they could talk), each one might say they are the real cat and the other is a fake cat. But in truth, the existence and validity of each cat is the same.

Extending the metaphor, I would like you to imagine that the cats are physical matter universes.

Each universe could be situated within its own compressed space time environment that allows for full interpenetration by another compressed physical matter universe through it, without collision or experience of being crowded out. Just like the two cats. Now that we have ticked the interpenetration box you are ready for "Many Worlds" and the Multiverse.

Creative Science - Everett's Multiverse

Hugh Everett was a brilliant American mathematician and quantum physicist in the 1950s. Everett was inspired to tackle the unsolved measurement problem in physics. He came up with a mathematically sound hypothesis that merged experience between the quantum and our physical macro-worlds. Everett's elegant theorem was seen as radical and out of keeping with the quantum/macro separation dualism established by the Copenhagen Interpretation, which was being taught in every university physics class around the world.

If you were to believe Everett's theory, then you no longer needed the Copenhagen mathematical appendices that were designed to plug the gap of the quantum/macro inconsistency that couldn't be explained. This caused Everett some problems because the Copenhagenists were successful physicists who dominated the world's physics think tanks and research facilities. Primary among this school was Niels Bohr, a Nobel prize winner in Physics who took personal issue with Everett's theory.

Feeling discriminated, bitter and suffering a marked lack of support for his paper, Everett vanished into physics obscurity and began working for defense contractors. It wasn't until 1967 that a group of physicists began to take Everett's work more seriously. They released a book that included Everett's full original dissertation called the *Many Worlds Interpretation of Quantum Mechanics,* and it was from this point that Everett's theory began to grow in scientific currency. Today, depending on whom you speak with, some physicists prefer to remain with the Copenhagen Interpretation and others are moving towards Many Worlds.

One of the biggest challenges to the greater adoption of Many Worlds is that while most physicists can understand the mathematics of it. They can't reconcile themselves with what it means for their everyday lives - that there are multiple copies of themselves running around in parallel universes.

For example, string theorist Juan Maldacena of the Institute for Advanced Study in Princeton, New Jersey says

> "When I think about the Everett (Many Worlds) Theory quantum mechanically, it is the most reasonable thing to believe. In everyday life, I do not believe it." (Byrne 2008)

And while some scientists have difficulty with the visualization process of Many Worlds, others don't. Most notably Steven Hawking, who in one of the last papers before his passing was fine-tuning his own version of the multiverse theory. (Sample 2018)

Now that we have covered the evolution of Many Worlds and the multiverse, we can return to look at the next part of our Creative Science framework called the theory of Probable Realities, a model that has Everett in mind.

Creative Science - Probable Realities

So, what do we mean by probable realities and why are they important for lucid dreamers?

Probable realities represent an ongoing explosion of sorts, a constant creation of new universes. Let's say we are invited to a dinner function. We wonder in our mind if we should go and in this instance we decide not to go. If we are asked the next day about what we did the night before we simply say we stayed at home.

Now the theory of probable realities would say, at the moment we decided to stay home, a spontaneous explosion of consciousness happened underneath our awareness. An explosion that led to the creation of a whole other universe that contains an Earth, with your house and an identical copy of you in it. If you're wondering where all these universes are, or how they fit alongside one another, you need to return to the concept of interpenetration that we covered in a previous section.

In that second universe, the other alternative is played out and you decide to attend the function. If we were to interview the "you" in the second universe, affectionately called a "probable you". That "you" would describe itself as the official you and not some ghostly offshoot of the real you. Just like the cat number two in our interpenetration example would think of itself as the real cat.

In other words, from the literally millions of probable "yous" out there in the universe on different probable "planet Earths", every single one of them would categorically say that they are the real deal. They would claim that their experience is the official story, and that all of the other "yous" are probable selves, from their perspective. In other words, Probability Theory helps us to understand that with each decision we make, we are seeding the creation of new universes all around us (Roberts 1979).

Why is this relevant for lucid dreaming?

It's relevant because in the dream state we can sometimes access the experiences or "goings on" of one of our probable selves. In other words, probable realities provide us with plausible, possible explanations for certain lucid dream events and experiences.

Creative Science - Time

Now that we have covered some probability theory we are going to continue our Creative Science framework by returning to our investigation of time.

Creative Science and our lucid-dreaming experience views past, present, and future as all co-existing simultaneously. For example, we would like you to consider the past as not being fixed. Intuitively this may feel like a strange concept. On the one hand, we can be open to the idea of a variety of possible futures, but on the other, we are less able to imagine how there could be more than one past?

If we return to our probability theory we will remember how each major decision made and not made is experienced in the full, spinning off into their own respective realities across many worlds. So, as we have possible futures, we also have multiple probable pasts.

Are there overlaps between the past, present and future? Or are they separated, hard dimensions that exist on their own?

Creative Science and our lucid dreaming experience would suggest they are mutually interdependent. So, changes in the past can affect present and future and equally changes in the future can ebb backwards to influence the present and the past.

Next, let's extend our Creative Science framework by introducing you to the idea of different "planes" of existence for lucid dreaming.

Creative Science - Planes of Existence

In this section, we will use the following terms interchangeably for simplicity's sake: universes, planes and dimensions.

The easiest way to start with this is to imagine a very large black hole in the shape of a dog. This black hole dog is so dense that anything coming near it gets sucked in and transformed by pressures so large that even light is altered by it. We could say that she's the top dog of the physical matter universe because she is so concentrated with matter.

Visualize now that you have been given a pair of inter-dimensional sunglasses that will allow your vision to see all the relevant planes, dimensions and universes that are possible. We now look again at our top dog black hole with our new glasses and see a smaller physical matter plane running through it, in the form of a white dog. Visualize that this white dog plane is at the other end of the matter spectrum, containing matter that is lighter and much less dense to what we are accustomed to on Earth.

Just as per the two cats in our section on interpenetration, our black dog cannot see the white dog and the white dog cannot see the black dog, yet they are both there. The black dog thinks the only type of universes that exist are the ones with dense matter like theirs. Similarly, the white dog thinks that the only planes that exist are lighter matter planes like theirs.

Now, if we take another look with our inter-dimensional sunglasses, we might see a very small and strange looking red bird universe interpenetrating the black dog and white dog universes.

In the red bird universe, matter is present in terms of something to look at, but it doesn't seem to have any physically measurable mass and behaves nothing like what we are used to on Earth, or in the black dog or white dog universes. On the red bird plane, matter seems to be following a different set of laws that are native and characteristic to that universe.

If we gave our inter-dimensional sunglasses to the black dog and the white dog and pointed out the red bird universe, the two dogs might say that the red bird plane is a non-matter universe. Because as far as the two dogs are concerned, nothing in the red bird universe has any mass in the sense of mass they are accustomed to.

If we gave the red bird inter-dimensional sunglasses to look at the black dog and white dog planes, the red bird may feel confused because he, she or it is not able to visually "put together" what is actually happening in these universes. As the red bird is only used to experiencing its own native framework and physics.

This little metaphor is to help you realize that as far as your lucid dreaming adventures are concerned, our physical matter-based universe, that contains Earth, is just one plane of existence among many. Furthermore, even though our physical body is located in this physical world, our wandering, lucid dreaming consciousness does not have to experience such limits and may materialize in a number of different planes, universes or dimensions from time to time.

From my experience, it is also true to say that differences in the environmental phenomena and dream-physics which are native to these planes and places can be highly disorienting and even confusing. Therefore, it is important to be mentally prepared to visit them with flexible expectations in advance.

Let's continue with our Creative Science adventure and launch into part two of the framework to understand some of the different "subtle body vehicles" that can carry our travelling consciousness during lucid dreams. We invite you to join us as we enthusiastically leap down the "rabbit hole" and would like to reiterate that the following ideas and concepts are a just framework for Creative Science and lucid dreaming. You'll get the most out of the next section if you don't become too caught up in judging right and wrong, real or unreal, and just use it as a visualization exercise. Contemplating subtle bodies and their characteristics is a good mental exercise to help scaffold thinking and prepare you for the high degree of variability in lucid dream experiences.

6. A Creative Science framework - Part 2

> "The further one goes, the less one knows" Lao Tzu

Creative Science - Physical Body Plane

In our lucid experience, your physical body seems to be interpenetrated by a number of other subtle bodies that all have their own micro-electromagnetic realities.

Subtle, because they seem to be made of fine material that is almost impossible to see with the naked eye, in most circumstances.

These subtle bodies form a network of support to "nourish" the physical body and also provide opportunities for your consciousness to free itself from the physical body from time to time, to rest and re-energize with experiences on other planes.

Creative Science - Etheric Body Plane

Your etheric body seems to be the closest subtle body to your physical body and is assisting with the transformation of energy from outside the body into usable forms for the body. The etheric body seems to hold a certain alignment with the physical body. For example, when you are doing any movement or motion it is moving as well. Slower stretching-based exercises such as Yoga and Tai Chi work directly with the etheric body and assist with its alignment, allowing for easier transformation of energy for the body's use.

In our experience, the etheric body has its own electromagnetic reality and can be damaged by physical trauma, bad weather and even overexposure to UV rays from the sun. In a lucid-dreaming context, working in the etheric body involves movement that is close to the ground, such as "glide-flying" where you push forward and glide a few centimeters/inches above the ground in a forwards or backwards motion.

Etheric plane dream environments seem to look the same, or very similar to our physical world. Sometimes etheric environments in lucid dreams carry a high level of viscosity, friction and resistance to movement. The etheric body seems to be affected by gravity at some level, less than our physical body but more than our astral body. The name the Ancient Egyptians gave to the etheric body was called the Ka (Grant 2019).

Creative Science - Astral Body Plane

The astral body seems to be made of finer material again and appears to be the seat of our emotions and desires. From our lucid dreaming experience, the astral body is one of the most heavily used dream bodies because it is often concerned with the emotional stabilization of the personality.

Many of us "normal" people who are living disciplined lives deny the expression of certain emotional drives. Lucid dreams in the astral body can facilitate a temporary outlet providing some relief to the psyche; whether it's making new friends, flying around in freedom, testing ideas or just participating in activated, emotional experiences. When it comes to environments, the astral plane is a gateway and cross-roads to many other planes and offers a fantastic diversity of lucid-dreaming experiences.

One of the most exciting features about the astral body is how you can use your own thought-power to achieve incredible things. Things that are very difficult to accomplish on Earth such as: moving large objects by thought-power alone, changing the appearance of an object, dematerializing or rematerializing your own form, inventing new objects and animating existing objects.

For example, on the astral, you can design your own house, think a car into reality and then scrap them both if you like and start over. As simple as that might sound, it's less easy to make things on the astral plane that can deliver a function. For instance, on the astral, it's harder to create a car that actually moves, as opposed to a static model of a car that doesn't. Astral environments seem to have a relationship with physical reality insofar that there are solid looking objects with some counterpart to the idea of mass, but they are not physically measurable.

In terms of dream-flying, the astral plane is the place where most of my lucid flying dreams have occurred. From leaping over buildings to shooting into outer space, travelling through walls or disappearing into some other plane, the astral has it all. In my experience, the astral subtle body is a very mobile and capable vehicle for lucid consciousness and can support travel across significant distances and also through time. The Ancient Egyptians called the astral body the Ba.

Creative Science - Inner Screen

Many of you will be wondering how we actually see in our dreams. The simplest way I can attempt to answer this question is that I appear to have some type of inner screen that is as bright and clear as any daytime scene. Onto this screen, some of my dream data is projected.

When it comes to lucid dreams, I find that they are most often experienced in the first person. I am literally moving through environments and experiencing events, first hand. This provides us with an odd hypothesis that it is possible to see lighted scenes in our lucid dreams, whilst our physical eyes are completely shut.

Scientists might say such dream scenes are merely a mishmash of recorded physical memories re-expressed for the purposes of dreaming. And I will be the first to admit that I have had some dreams in that category where it seems more of a creative artwork of recorded memories. But the dreams I am going to present to you in the pages that follow do not fall into this category and, instead, represent lucid live journeys into a truly odd variety of places and spaces.

7. My Lucid Dream Journal

> "I am one of those who think like Nobel, that humanity will draw more good than evil from new discoveries." Physics Nobel Laureate, Marie Curie

> "Whatever you see in existence, both moving and unmoving, is only the combination of the field of activities and the knower of the field." Bhagavad-gita 13.27

Electrical
Friday, 15 November 2002 - Lucid Out of Body Experience

I had a greasy meal before bed and woke up at 3:30 am and couldn't get back to sleep. At 6 am, I felt an urgency to sleep and worried about not being able to perform at work. As I finally slipped into sleep, I felt a warm wellness and familiarity - I was about to leave my body. I was a little more conscious/lucid than usual, so I decided to use this opportunity to practice my technique. As I popped out of my body, I felt a charged feeling that was distinctly electrical. I could fly upwards in the room easily at will, but flying down to the ground with accuracy was harder and more clumsy. It did not feel like I was doing this inside my normal physical body but more as an electrical field of sensitivity and awareness.

Flight Notes:

If I'm having trouble falling asleep and there are only a few hours left before wake up, sometimes my consciousness seems to dump other processes that were previously organized. Moving into a state of urgency, my lucid consciousness focuses on getting out of my physical body as fast as possible to allow the necessary re-energizing to take place before I wake up. Sometimes lucid dream experiences can happen when the body is at a high level of exhaustion. Nonetheless, I would not recommend artificially creating exhaustion in the hope of becoming lucid more frequently, as out-of-body lucid experiences can occur just as easily when one is enjoying a good night's sleep.

Stairs
Monday, 5 November 2004 – Lucid Flying Dream

I began the lucid dream on top of some wooden stairs. It was a big, open hall and I flew down from the top flight of stairs to the other parts of the room by angling myself and pushing, using my mind. The sensation was very much like gliding.

Flight Notes:

The control of your body on the bed whilst you are dreaming seems to play a role in making certain adjustments when you are flying. For example, I have had dreams where I have had to lay incredibly still with my physical body on the bed to maintain a flight trajectory in the dream. Having said this, I would recommend against anyone strapping themselves to their bed to try and artificially stop their body from moving, as this can cause temperature control problems, making unpleasant lucid dreams more likely.

The River
Saturday, 26 March 2005 – Lucid Flying Dream

It had been a good night of lucid dreaming, but now I had a distinct realization that it was time to wake up. In order to make this happen inside the dream, I found myself approaching a river, which needed to be crossed. I ran along the bank looking for a narrow place to jump and found the perfect spot. I then dashed up to the edge and jumped. The sensation of flight was fantastic. Not only did I jump over the river, but so much further that I had to adjust my speed and brake towards the end of arc so I could land properly.

Flight Notes:

The sensation of flight speed in such jumps is a little slowed down compared to what we might be used to in the physical world. At the point of leaping there is a reduced gravity at work, so you push off as normal but instead find yourself flying much higher and further. On this occasion, there was no flap of wind at my face as some astral environments don't seem to have "air" in the terms we are used to on Earth. If you can visualize jumping in a reduced gravity environment like an astronaut on the moon, you would be getting close to the experience.

Experiments
Monday, 2nd of January 2006 – Lucid Flying Dream

I was lucid dreaming and decided to practice flying in a room with very high ceilings. There were a number of other people in the room, including one young woman in particular with dark hair, who was taking an interest in my progress. I practiced flying up to the top of the room using different thought patterns. The first thought command was to fly forwards whilst thrusting my hands in the "superman style", which seemed to work fine. On my second attempt, I used the same thought command but this time without any superman forward hand thrust and it worked just as well. So, the flying seemed to be mostly about *mental control*. I tried fast ascent. I tried slow ascent. I tried slow descent. I noted that it was difficult to determine the speed of ascent after rebounding from a descent. One thing I tried many times but was unable to master, was being able to hover motionless in the air holding a fixed position.

Flight Notes:

The astral environment doesn't exhibit a single physics, but rather seems to be a collective environment of different planes each one with its own native physics. In most of these astral micro-environments gravity is lower than Earth gravity and the structure of certain types of matter can be manipulated by thought, as a general rule. Despite these apparent consistencies, the experiences of inertia and friction seem to be highly variable and dependent on which universe or plane you find yourself in.

Reverse Gravity
Saturday, 11 February 2006 – Lucid Flying Dream

I'm at a busy traffic junction and then all of a sudden, I'm rising up into the air. I am very conscious and actively trying to control the rate of my ascent and would like to level out and stop rising. But to no avail, because I keep on rising fast whilst looking down at the little traffic junction that is becoming smaller and smaller below me. Finally, there is a point where I stop rising, well beyond the clouds and a significant distance above the ground.

Flight Notes:

In the astral, when you are low and close to the ground, it can feel that there is a type of weak gravity effect. Once you start rising, it's as though gravity is working in reverse so that it's easier to go higher than it is to propel yourself downwards or forwards. When you look down at the world below, it's normal to have an emotional reaction that goes something like, "Oh my God, how am I going to get back down?"

Despite the shock, there's really no cause for worry because in lucid dreaming there is no hard impact on reaching the ground like there is on Earth. If you manage to fly down, you just peacefully level out until you come to a comfortable stop, or if you can't be bothered flying down, there is a shortcut available - just wake up!

Precision Flying
Sunday, 26 March 2006 – Lucid Flying Dream

I was standing with a group of people under a tree. I decided to levitate upwards and landed firmly balanced on top of a fence, which on the face of it doesn't sound amazing, but produced a strong sense of satisfaction for me in the dream as I had learned a new controlled-flying skill.

Flight Notes:

Lucid flying dreams provide opportunities to test and try new skills that help you develop a sense of progress and achievement. Precision-flying may sound easy but it isn't, as many lucid flight environments have an *astral current* of sorts. This astral current isn't visible but exerts a force or influence on your flight path just like an ocean current affects the progress of a boat.

I haven't been able to work out if this astral current is an astral counterpart of Earth-based wind or whether it is some other force entirely. What I do know from experience is if your precision-flight is working in a different direction to the current, then it is going to be more challenging and you are likely to use more brain chemical fuel, per unit of distance covered. In this dream, the current was negligible, providing an excellent environment for my hover on top of the fence.

Glide Flying Layer
Saturday, 21 October 2006 – Lucid Flying Dream

I started flying high and fast. Returning to Earth, I was coming down more slowly, but this time was able to accelerate to a pinpoint stop a few centimeters/inches above the ground, without suffering any momentum transfer. Which I found strange and suggests that the mass of my astral body in physical terms may be negligible. The ground below me had some moss and lichen on its surface that was very similar to the ground outside of our house in winter.

Flight Notes:

In some astral and etheric environments there seems to be a layer about a foot above the ground that works like a friction-less belt. You can land on it, you can glide along it, all without actually touching the ground. When I make use of the term "glide-flying" I am talking about gliding along this close-to-ground layer. The sensation is quite amazing.

CSF Swimming
Friday, 10 February 2006 – Lucid Flying Dream

I woke up at 4:30 am, laid in bed for about two hours and then had a lucid dream at 6:30 am. I was walking down a footpath with wind on my face while a car passed me in the background. Noises were perfect in their perspective, like I was in an Earth environment. Suddenly I took off like a jet soaring through the air, feeling the wind resistance. A few moments later, I'm looking down at the clouds and caught myself thinking that I was really there, flying out of the body in physical space. For some reason on this occasion, I have an exceptionally lucid and clear memory of the returning period to waking consciousness that occurred in three stages.

One, in the present I am flying above the clouds looking down at Earth. Two, I descend into amazingly clear water in which, somehow, I'm able to breathe. Three, at the bottom of the crystal clear water is a very large dark-colored mass, and I feel emotionally *drawn* towards it.

My curiosity gets the better of me and I dive down lower to explore it. Very close, I reach out with my hand to touch it and on contact wake up instantaneously, realizing that the dark mass was in fact my brain, that I had returned to!

Flight Notes:

This is one of only three lucid dreams where I have literally seen my own brain. On this occasion, I am returning after a lucid dream-induced out-of-body experience and one thing I can tell you is that the scale of my returning consciousness (me) was very small compared to the size of my brain.

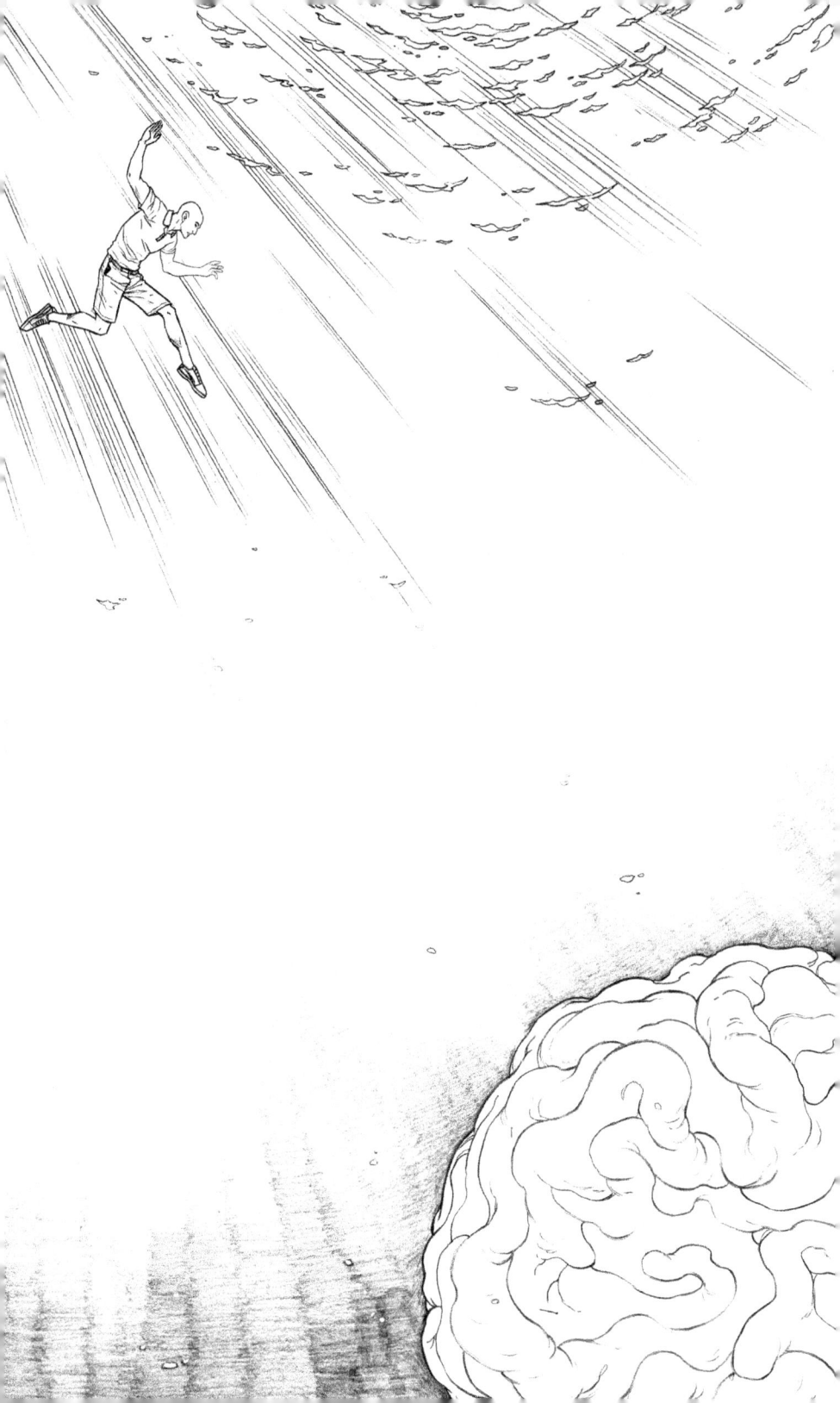

Bellows Breath flying
Tuesday, 1 January 2008 - Lucid Flying Dream

This was a flight dream with a significant difference. Unlike my manually controllable, brain chemical-induced, short, flying dreams. This one was very difficult to control. In addition, the orders of magnitude and travel distance far exceeded that which I was accustomed to. On this occasion, the simple act of deep inhalation over three successive breaths, one after the other, shot me up so fast and so far, that by the third breath, I found myself looking down and seeing almost the whole planet Earth below me.

Flight Notes:

I have only ever experienced this type of flight once. I am not sure what event in the dream triggered me to take three consecutive breaths, as my lucidity started only a second or so before my first big flight breath. People interested in using out-of-body experiences for space exploration may be interested to experiment with such breath-generated lucid transport.

Brain Chemical Fuel Tank
Wednesday, 5 December 2007- Lucid Flying Dream

I was at a music concert. The speed was exhilarating. I flew for what seemed like 400m in a curving trajectory at around 60-70 kms per hour, with very clear vision. All of a sudden, I felt myself slowing and realized my brain chemical flying fuel was spent. In the end, I tried one levitation of just a few meters and couldn't even manage it - my flying fuel tank was empty. I found it interesting that whatever this brain chemical lucid-flying fuel is, it certainly seems to be in limited supply.

Flight Notes:

The chemical fuel that is used to support lucid-flight seems to be made up of certain healthy minerals, proteins in the blood and also brain chemical by products that are left over after other brain processes. In this way, lucid dream flying can put these left over chemicals and minerals to good use effectively cleaning the brain and the cerebrospinal fluid that your brain floats in. These flight chemicals and minerals appear to gradually build-up over time, making lucid flight experiences not an every night event.

Astral Bike Ride
Friday, 8 May 2009 – Lucid Flying Dream

I was riding my bike on the way to visit some friends in the dream. I was conscious of the fact that the bike I was riding had been built with my own thought patterns, i.e. an astral bike. The traffic was quite busy and I had a little trouble turning around, but eventually was pedaling quickly and making good lane choices.

As my speed increased, the dream built to a crescendo where I and another fellow riding next to me, jumped our bikes into the air. As we leaped upwards, I was very conscious that my own thought-power during the jump was impacting on the rate of my ascent. Eventually we reached the top of our ascent and leaned back on the bikes ready for descent. I landed without damage to me, but the bike was broken beyond repair. I remember thinking that I would need to "will together" another bike, which I quickly tried to do on the spot, but was unable to.

Flight Notes:

My difficulty with recreating my bike using thought-power is not an isolated experience on the astral. Sometimes the astral environment doesn't respond in the way you would like it to because there are complexities that you have not discovered.

It can take time to create some objects, which may be time that you do not have because you want to wake up and cut from the lucid dream. Or perhaps the thought-force of your will is not suited to the object you are trying to create? Or maybe you can muster the thought-force but can't identify the right pattern for the object? Or maybe you can create the object but do not have the extra mental resources available to animate it? It's not as though you can appear on the astral and build the Taj Mahal in a few seconds. Most of the more impressive-looking structures I have encountered on the astral, seem to have been built up over a period of time and reinforced by repeated thought patterns. You can tend to your astral "dream home" in much the same way as someone would water their garden or renovate their home on earth. The repetition of the thought-force strengthens the integrity of the astral object, giving it an impression of permanence and identity.

Astral Car
Thursday, 14 May 2009 - Lucid Dream

In my dream, I looked through the window of my house at an astrally-created sporty, red car. On impulse, I decided to see whether I could affect the body and appearance of the car using my will only. I concentrated energy from the center of my forehead and sent a strong thought-beam aimed at the car. For the first few seconds nothing happened. But then the car began to puncture, warp and finally exploded into flames! By the end it was so burnt out and ruined that I felt a little guilty, but I knew all was not lost because with the right conditions and enough time, I would be able to create something else.

Flight Notes:

There can be a slight delay or lag in the astral between the execution of a certain thought and the reaction of matter to that thought. In other words, it seems to take matter in the astral a few seconds to translate or interpret your thoughts before the relevant object or objects spring into response.

The Wall
Thursday, 4 February 2010 – Lucid Flying Dream

In this lucid flying dream, my vision was remarkably clear. I rose up into the air and began to direct myself towards a thick, plasterboard wall. For some reason I had the desire to pass through the wall. Without having any distinct technique, I moved to the wall and slowly began to pass through it without any pain. To my surprise, this was achieved not so much by putting myself through the wall, but by pulling the wall through a small area in the center of my forehead. The texture of the plaster moving through my forehead felt very strange and "chalky". Then I found myself clear and on the other side, without any damage to the wall.

Flight Notes:

When we travel from A to B, we like to think of A and B as stationary points and ourselves as the object that moves. In the astral, it's possible to travel between point A and point B whilst you are stationery. If you are standing at point A (on one side of a wall) you can get to point B (on the other side) by pulling the space between points A and B through you. So, by the end of the experience you are standing on the other side of the wall, yet you have hardly moved.

I had another interesting lucid dream on the same night.

China Café
Thursday, 4 February 2010 - Lucid Dream

In the dream I found myself in a cafe somewhere in China. Below me were a group of three Chinese men sitting together doing a business deal in a restaurant. I was hovering above them and seemed to be immersed in a watery liquid, which moved all around me but was clear at the base, where it separated into the air above the men. This made it easy for me to view them. The closest experience I can relate it to is looking through a glass-bottomed boat. But instead of being in a boat, I'm in a watery animated fluid, suspended directly above the men.

The vision and sense experiences were totally visceral, as if I had projected to a real place and moment in physical reality, via my lucid dream. I was feeling very self-conscious, thinking that even though the men would not likely be able to see me, that they could perhaps sense my presence.

As I manipulated around the room above them, I did send out a single mental thought letting them know I was there, for reasons of etiquette, and also for the scientific tester in me, who wondered if any of them would sense my presence? Almost immediately, my heart stopped as one of the men looked straight up at me. However, the look on his face indicated he was not able to see me.

Flight Notes:

I have only had this type of experience a few times in nearly 20 years. Each time I felt as though I was physically there, along with a sense of embarrassment and unannounced intrusion. In my experience, such visits seem to be spontaneous and random. In terms of "getting to China" I don't remember any lucid-flying. I was just there in the Chinese café without any lucid memory of how I got there.

Here's another interesting dream that occurred on the same night!

Levitation
Thursday, 4 February 2010 – Lucid Flying Dream

I found myself doing a variety of exercises in levitation, including one where I was able to fly upside down towards the ground and precision stop, just before my head hit a bathtub. It took me about four attempts to get this right, after which a buzzer went off somewhere in the background apparently indicating that I'd completed the assigned task? Later, I found myself in a printing factory and moving my arms in a tai-chi type of movement through a clear and highly viscous atmosphere that felt like water, but in which I experienced no breathing difficulties.

Flight Notes:

Precision stops seem to be quite difficult to master. The bell going off in the background was symbolic of a test being undertaken. I have experienced many other lucid dreams where I felt like a test participant. Sometimes on passing a test the dream will offer a reward.

As for the printing factory in the second part of the lucid dream - over time and through successive lucid experiences, you can gradually develop a lucid dream symbology where certain recurring symbols help you better understand your dreams. For example financial growth is sometimes represented to me in lucid dreams as a water phenomenon with positive financial opportunities appearing as clear water and negative financial opportunities as dirty and turbid water. We will be spending more time working with you on the science of lucid dream interpretation in our next book *Creative Science and Visualization*.

Ocean Promenade
Wednesday, 3 November 2010 – Lucid Flying Dream

First, some back story:

On the day before the dream, I had been in meetings in a regional West Australian town called Carnarvon. At the end of the day, I met with some friends at a harborside café before flying into Perth to stay at a hotel on Scarborough Beach.

In the morning immediately following the dream, I delivered a workshop presentation to some colleagues in Perth CBD. The meeting also included others tuning in by teleconference from Melbourne.

And now the dream:

I was standing in the morning light at the front of the hotel on the promenade next to the beach. The ocean was in the background. People were walking towards me across the grass and concrete paths on their way to buses, trains and workplaces. It would have been an ordinary morning scene, except there was a tremendous force of superimposed bliss over everything.

The closest person to me was a young man with dark, curly hair in his early to mid-20s. There was a type of depression or haze hanging around him, but the area directly above his head showed a pure white light. This was a big shock to me because even though I had read about auras and the theory relating to them, I'd never seen one before. I then looked around and realized that I was able to see the auras of every single person walking on all sides of me. The auras were of different colors, shapes and sizes. I noticed a lot of white light and beautiful rainbow colors everywhere and spiritual warmth. In short, it was a world of bliss, an experience of heaven on Earth. It lasted for about 12 seconds. Then it was gone.

Next, I was able to take off into the sky using the force of one hand. I found myself flying towards the city of Perth. The speed of flight was blindingly fast and seemed to last much longer than my own brain chemicals usually allowed for, giving me the idea that this particular flight was being "assisted."

Next, I found myself in a building, giving a presentation in a workshop room. It was the same workshop room that I would find myself presenting in, a few hours later on the following morning, even though I had never been there before.

In the lucid dream, at some point during the live workshop presentation, I found myself entering the teleconference connected phone that was lying on the meeting table. I experienced a slow down with a peculiar metallic feeling as I pushed myself inside the metal phone line. I could palpably feel the hardness and cold of it moving through my forehead. This was accompanied by a stretching noise or vibration. I then came out the other side and found myself walking around a business office, somewhere in Melbourne. I was hugely embarrassed and concerned that I would be discovered by someone, so I quickly made myself scarce and woke up back in my Scarborough Beach Hotel room. Sitting bolt upright, I noticed that the balcony screen door to my room was slightly open, allowing the sea breeze to creep into the room.

Flight Notes:

In moving along the phone line, there was a distinct similarity with the process I used to move through the wall in the lucid dream "The Wall" Thursday, 4 February 2010. In both cases I had been able to travel through matter by moving material through the center of my forehead. In the wall dream I could feel the texture of the plaster. In this dream it was like moving a cold steel cable through the center of my forehead producing strange physical sensations associated with the cold "taste" of the metal.

Some of you will be wondering what I meant in the dream description by saying my flight felt like it was being "assisted?" Over the years, I have had a few lucid dreams where my flight speed far eclipses what I am usually able to generate using my brain chemical fuel-based travel. In some of these "warp speed" occasions I have perceived certain "angelic" beings, who for one reason or another, have decided that I need to be "shown something" and have taken it upon themselves to do the showing. Mostly these beings seem to choose to do the assisting without being seen. I'm led to believe such senior roles require the giving of service unconditionally, without any expectation of thanks or return benefit. But occasionally, they may reveal part of themselves. Without the assistance of such selfless and loving beings, I doubt that I would have accumulated so much content to bring to you. And so, in this note, I am going to quietly honor their silent contribution to my inner development.

Back to Class
Sunday, 15 May 2011 – Lucid Flying Dream

I decided to horizontal "glide-fly" along the corridor of a hospital ward that felt like a familiar place to me. At the end of the glide-fly, I approached a classroom of students and a lecturer. I had a feeling that I had been there before. I took my place in a student's chair making much of my controlled transition into the chair by a single fluid movement.

Flight Notes:

You may or may not be studying something in your daily physical life right now but there are also many education activities and events occurring on the astral. Sometimes a formal environment like this could be an astral counterpart of an actual physical, learning environment, or equally it could be just an astral meeting place to discuss a certain topic of interest.

Pre-Flight Brain Reactions
Wednesday, 8 June 2011 – Lucid Flying Dream

I stayed up until 10:30 pm and subsequently slept solidly until 4 am. I then found myself lucid dreaming and was presented with a living model of my brain in action. I was positioned behind my head. My skull and brain cells did not obstruct the view, and I was able to see through my whole brain.

Incredibly fascinated, I watched a chain reaction occur in my brain that began at the back of my head in the left hemisphere and continued in a series of reactions working around the left edge all the way to the front of the left hemisphere. The reactions then continued across and into the front of my right hemisphere and stopped. This chain reaction was presented to me as small, electrical, consecutive explosions related to the out-of-body projection that followed.

I soon found myself lucid dream-flying over a roadway. I had the distinct feeling that I could have shot straight up into the sky if that had been a priority, however I was more fascinated and distracted by the insight that I was given just prior to take-off.

Flight Notes:

This lucid dream was quite significant for me because it provided insight about potential pre-condition reactions in the brain that may help to support lucid flight. Of particular and odd interest was why my pre-flight brain reactions began at the back of the left hemisphere and ran along the left edge, to the front left and then across to the front of the right hemisphere? This could suggest that, hemispherically speaking, some parts of the brain may be more involved with out-of-body projections and lucid flight than others, at least to begin with.

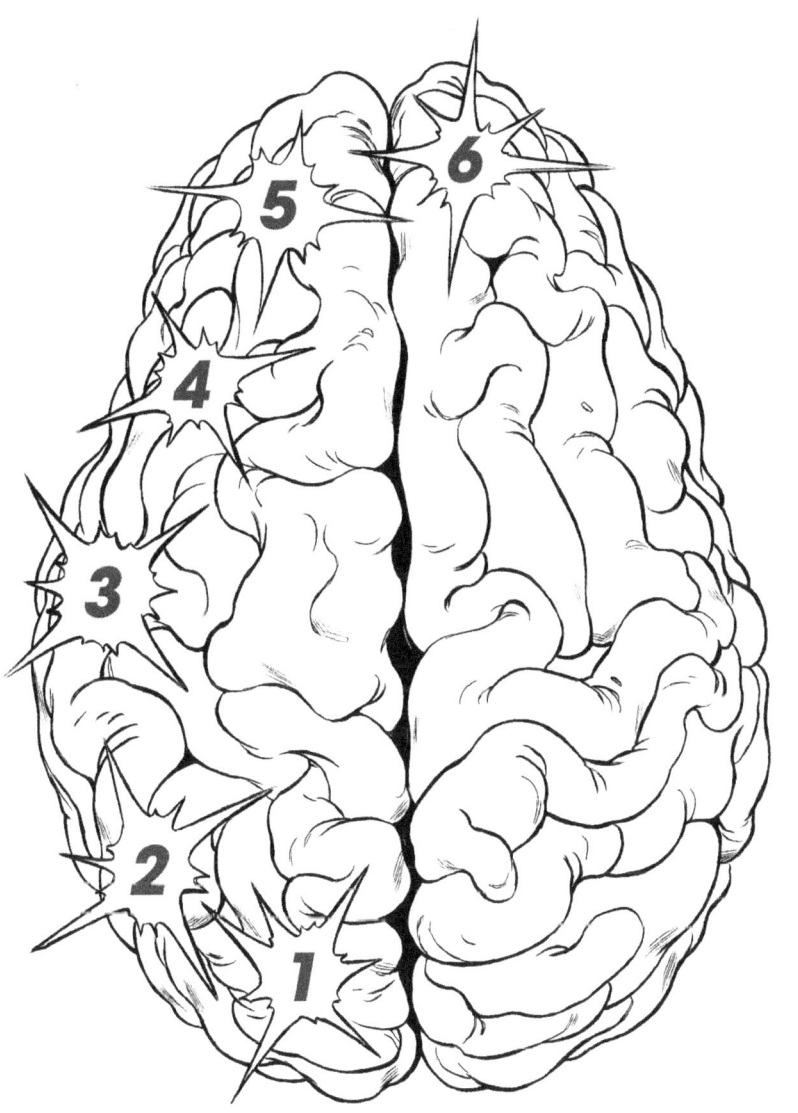

Reflections
Sunday, 12 June 2011 - Lucid Dream

I was travelling back from a beach house and noticed that I had the choice of flying or glide-walking above the ground. Both seemed as easy as each other. Although, it was challenging to maintain low altitude with control.

Flight Notes:

Some patterns are beginning to emerge in my lucid flying dreams as follows:

- Flying straight up (direct ascent) - easiest
- Flying forward - possible but expensive in brain chemical fuel (reduced flight distance and time)
- Hovering stationary in a fixed position - difficult
- Controlled descent or down-flying - very difficult to control and master.

After many years, to my great relief, I finally discovered that down-flying could be made easier by tipping yourself, that is your body in flight, upside down in the dream. This strikes me as odd, yet I have tested it a number of times since and it seems to hold true. It also brings up two more questions: One, why does one's orientation whilst projecting in a lucid dream (i.e. upside down or right side up), impact on the control of vertical flight? Two, how does the up or down orientation of the astral body relate to the position of the dreamer's physical or other subtle bodies back in the bedroom? Hopefully one of my readers will solve these two questions and write me with the answer.

Action Potential
Sunday, 5 February 2012 – Lucid Flying Dream

I was flying out through the glass door of a large office complex and some people were asking me how I was able to do it. I replied "It is an action potential that builds up over time." On this particular instance during the flight, I felt I had enough flight power to carry someone with me so they could experience it also, although I completed the flight on my own.

Flight Notes:

The feeling before lucid flight is now so familiar that either I intuitively recognize the preconditions for flight, or I literally see a flight-ready version of myself arrive or appear in the dream and I transfer my consciousness into that subtle body.

Viscosity 1
Sunday 29 April 2012 – Lucid Flying Dream

I found myself lucid dreaming in a very viscous section of the etheric plane. Moving through it was like moving through a thick heavy, watery, jelly-like substance. I had to use a swimming motion with my arms but breathing wasn't a problem. There were some other people immersed in the substance along with me, all doing their best to navigate through it as well. Some parts of the dream scenery displayed design elements from the trees and foliage along the jogging path, that I would experience the following morning.

Flight Notes:

When looking across all of my lucid dreams there are a number of content themes emerging; people, places and emotions seem to have the biggest impact on lucid dream content. That isn't to say if you are not going to interesting places, doing work with interesting people, or experiencing powerful emotions, that you won't have interesting lucid dreams. However as a rule of thumb, I have found as you become involved in events with greater numbers of people or equally, people with strong emotions and forces of will, then the greater the psych-based "charge" for your related lucid dream activity.

Viscosity 2
Wednesday, 2 May 2012 - Lucid Dream

I woke up at 3:57 am and then slowly slipped back to sleep with increased consciousness. I was with two people practicing to see if I could learn how to do the double-back somersault that is performed by gymnasts.

Flight Notes:

In etheric lucid dream environments, there is sometimes extra friction caused by a thicker, viscous atmosphere that is more liquid-based than the gas-based air we are used to, surrounding us on Earth. This "liquid" resistance is handy for learning acrobatic maneuvers because your body weight is supported and the velocity of movement is slower. A similar and useful visualization is watching how quickly a party balloon decelerates with air friction after it is struck so that it looks like the balloon "stalls" in the air. In the etheric, it is you stalling in the viscous ether atmosphere.

In Dual
Saturday 5th May 2012 - Lucid Dream

At the beginning of falling asleep, I noticed a strange feeling in my hands and the sense of being "in dual". In other words, the transfer out of my physical body was not complete, so my lucid consciousness was in my physical body and my astral body at the same time.

In the dream, I found myself in a field with some large white birds. Some of them were territorial and tried to peck at me. So I took off and began to fly headfirst and flat on my tummy. I had a feeling of energy that I could go wherever I wanted, but as I did not have a clear objective in mind, the opportunity passed.

I then found my conscious awareness had switched back into my body lying in bed. Thinking my dream was over, I viewed the familiar layout of my bedroom around me. Suddenly, I realized that the bedroom wall opposite me was missing and in its place was a three-dimensional blue sky. So, I am staring at this "blue sky" that has taken the place of my bedroom wall and assume that I must be still dreaming. I see a cloudy mist gather in the blue sky in front of me that takes the rough shape of a person. I am watching this person-shaped mist intently, wondering what is going to happen next.

Then, a life-sized version of me, materializes from the cloud mist, confidently walks straight up to the bed and then merges with my physical body, at which point I'm fully physically awake and feeling "blown away" by the event.

Flight Notes:

The feeling of being "in dual" is reasonably common, yet for some people it can be frightening if they aren't able to fully understand what is happening to them. Simply explained, it is possible for your lucid consciousness to expand and stretch across your physical body and your subtle bodies at the same time.

The Shoe
Saturday, 29 September 2012 - Lucid Dream

I am walking along a street with a woman and a young man. For some reason, I became aware of a twitching or glitching down by the young man's feet. Upon closer inspection, his shoes were switching from runners into female high heels and then back into runners before my eyes. I stood there, realizing that such an event was not possible in a physical environment. Becoming more lucid, I turned to the woman and said "Do you know what? I'm dreaming!" On this occasion, the emotional surge and additional lucidity caused me to pop right out of the dream and I woke up.

Flight Notes:

The criterion method is one technique you can use to "wake yourself up" inside the dream. By identifying dream elements that don't make sense, and bringing yourself into a higher state of lucidity. Just try to control your emotions or otherwise you can bump out of your dream, as I did here.

Long Distance Flight
Tuesday, 26 March 2013- Lucid Flying Dream

I sensed the energy to fly and took off with a set task in mind to break my own record for horizontal flight distance. I wanted to see if I could fly to Kangaroo Island in South Australia from my (former) home in suburban Prospect (Adelaide). I made good progress but found it challenging to redirect thought-force so that I could move forwards instead of straight up. The dream physics of flying forward was challenging in this dream because there was a stronger sideways astral current to contend with. The direction of the current was working against my progress, making it easier for me to hold a fixed position, than fly forwards.

So, I began instead to lead with my left hand in-flight. This subtle rebalancing had the desired effect and I was able to make some more progress. By the time I ran out of fuel I had fallen well short of my intended destination but still felt a sense of satisfaction ending up on a rocky outcrop at the top of a beach next to a line of black rocks that went all the way to the water's edge.

Flight Notes:

When a pilot flies a passenger aircraft in the physical world, he or she makes adjustments to compensate for wind direction, sideways drift, altitude and so on. When you are flying in the astral you will also sometimes need to make adjustments to maintain a stable trajectory of flight.

In this case, leading with my left hand in the dream assisted the rebalancing process to make best use of the conditions. So, we have seen that the relative position of the subtle body can affect your astral flight dynamics, whether you are standing up or upside down, leaning to one side and so on.

Equally, there have been other times when the position of my astral subtle body seems less important than the mental and emotional thought-force that is powering the flight. Changes to the application and direction of this thought-force can itself compensate for flow-dynamics alterations that you are making to the "aircraft" or subtle body.

Another way of visualizing this is instead of an aircraft pilot on Earth altering the trim of flight by moving the wing or tail flaps, he or she can also alter flight trajectory by adjusting the jet engine throttle directly.

In a lucid flying dream on the astral plane the jet engine providing thrust is your own thought force. The only limitation in my experience is that due to the brain chemical fuel required, it's not possible to fly for extended periods at high speed. For example, if you are happy to "drift" and go easy on the fuel you might sustain a longer flight. On the other hand, if you are wanting to travel blazingly fast then you can do so, but expect that your fuel is going to be spent faster.

River Redgum
Sunday, 30 March 2014 - Lucid Flying Dream

This lucid dream occurred the night before I left on a trip to a country town called Collarenbri in New South Wales. I found myself very high up in a white house overlooking a crystalline ocean. It was truly amazing, like a scene out of a Hollywood movie. I placed my hand on the window and it felt warm. I knew intuitively that I could either stay and enjoy the view, or move out of this floating house through the window, which I did.

This brought me into a slow motion skydive above a crystal clear ocean. I could move my body and change the angle of the slow dive, one way or another. For a while I dived downwards but then, as I neared the water's surface, I found myself making a slow motion deceleration and then I suddenly jumped to another setting next to a beautiful gumtree on a river shore.

Flight Notes:

In my lucid dreaming experience, there are trees and then there are trees. I have experienced special trees in the astral environment that are counterparts of trees that look tired or even physically dead on Earth. Yet on the astral, they function as doorways and bringers of information from far away.

A number of my flying dreams have also been linked to leaps in my personal growth. For example, on the night before an exciting new project, the chances of a lucid-flying dream are always higher. This could suggest that lucid-flying dreams can be linked to improvements in our own progress and opportunities in physical life.

Pre-Flight Rocking
Saturday, 10 January 2014 Lucid Dream

I woke up in the morning but wanted to experience some more deep sleep and get right out of my body to fully replenish and rejuvenate myself. I began to doze and felt a distinct shrinking into a body that was smaller than my physical body. Straight away my consciousness in this little body began shuttling back and forth about 30 centimeters above my physical body. It was a very peculiar feeling. The rate of rocking became faster and seemed to be building up to something, but because I was physically awake my lucid consciousness couldn't fully "break free".

Flight Notes:

What I noticed about being in this smaller body is that it still felt like "me" as I rocked back and forth. Familiar physical feelings such as motion, a changing center of gravity and even a touch of vertigo were all part of the experience. The rocking of my subtle body did not need constant thought-force to maintain, although I could use my thinking to slow down or speed up the rocking. It felt like a process or program that I had started up by some means to release my lucid consciousness.

Lucid Eye Experiments
Saturday, 21 June 2014 - Lucid astral creative practice

I was lucid dreaming and looking at my own reflection in the mirror. I was able to change the color of my eyes at will. I asked for blue eyes and then it happened. I was able to play around with the intensity, expression and look of my eyes. This was a very enjoyable, creative and fun astral practice.

Flight Notes:

You don't have to be flying across the sky to have fun with lucid-dreaming. Simple little astral exercises like this can be extremely entertaining and worthwhile. In my experience, you can significantly control your appearance in the astral and the way you appear to others. But it's also true to say that people who are suitably skilled can see through such a veneer. Ultimately, how you appear to others in your astral subtle body relates to your own ideas about yourself including health, illness, fitness and even the things that you spend a lot of time thinking about. If your mind is full of grubby thoughts, then this may be reflected in your astral appearance. Conversely, if you are living a life that involves the selfless helping of others, then your astral image can shimmer with crystal clear white light.

Words In The Sky
Saturday, 19 July 2014 - Lucid Flying Dream

I was lucid dream-flying and noticed a curving parabolic arc of words in a fixed position in the sky. I wanted to get closer and read the contents of one of the paragraphs. I was able to change my flight direction by a small left to right manipulation of my left eye. As I came up close to the words, I remember reading some of them in the dream, but for some reason I didn't feel the urgency to fully wake up and write the words down.

Flight Notes:

Sometimes you will come across distinct and clear messages in lucid dreams, such as words, letters and the like. It might be just a flash of text or it could be a prolonged viewing of a statement. There have been times I have woken myself up and written down the text because I felt it could be important, and other times where I was frankly too tired.

Back Flying Innovation!
Tuesday, 8 April 2014 - Lucid Flying Dream

I'm lucid dream-walking down the road in metropolitan Hobart on the island of Tasmania and decide to do some low level glide-flying parallel to the street. I begin to levitate whilst facing forwards but quickly become agitated as I take off vertically at speed. I didn't want any vertical trajectory on this occasion. But this wasn't working out very well and I had a lot of difficulty controlling my height. I then stopped and turned my body so that my back was facing in the direction of travel.

With that simple change I instantly improved my altitude control and felt relieved as I lowered to hover a couple of feet above the ground. I then took off for a second time and began to fly quite fast "back first" along the road. For some reason I was not worried about bumping into anything. The "back flying" had minor vertical lift to begin with and then leveled out into a stable, horizontal trajectory whilst I was standing upright in a fixed position. I was consciously aware that I could increase my speed a little more, from the roughly 20 to 30 kmph that I seemed to be traveling, before my brain chemical fuel ran out.

Flight Notes:

The discovery of 'back-first' flying was a key turning point in my lucid dream-flying technique that solved my altitude control problems. The flooding sense of relief I felt in fixing such a long-standing problem was only temporary, as three other perplexing questions quickly entered my mind.

Why should a change in the direction that my astral body is facing make it easier for me to control my vertical height? Flying, standing upright, is terribly un-aerodynamic, because the whole of your body is in resistance to the direction of travel, so why have I found it possible to fly fast in this manner? Does flying back-first in the direction of travel say something about the astral or subtle body machinery that is involved?

I hope that my readers will experiment along these lines and send me their insights.

Hidden Things
Wednesday, 18 March 2015 - Lucid Flying Dream

I was dreaming with a very high degree of lucidity and leapt into the air with the least amount of energy and emotion possible, as I didn't want to bump out of the dream. The beginning of the flight was more of a glide fly near to the ground and then I rose to just above building height.

At this higher altitude, the impact of gravity departed and I was able to project horizontally with ease. I could clearly feel the cool night air and was in an investigational mood looking for anomalies and things that might be there, but are not fully visible, yet may have left some type of recognizable signature.

Flight Notes:

There have been many times whilst lucid dreaming that I have chanced upon something small that looks odd. A strange light, a weird refraction, a cup out of place, a faint face in the forest, or something else that doesn't make sense. In lucid dream environments this can often mean that some-*thing* is there, but you are not able to see the thing fully because it is sitting in another plane. It could be that 5% of the object is visible in the plane you are on and 95% is on a different plane. Sometimes, to solve such intriguing puzzles, I have had to play astral detective and produce a new subtle body from the material of the plane that I want to see and then transfer my consciousness into that body. Having achieved this, all of a sudden, the hidden object or item becomes fully visible.

Astral Telekinesis 1
Thursday, 9 July 2015 – Lucid Flying Dream

I was driving a car full of well-behaved men using my willpower. The car took off into the air and was able to fly. It was tricky guiding it with my will and difficult to keep the car on a straight trajectory.

Flight Notes:

Moving objects on the astral is something anyone can do given the right circumstances. I found this particular dream interesting because the astral sometimes works as a type of testing ground, before things can be brought into physical reality.

For example, if you are contemplating a certain complex action in the physical, such as negotiating an important business agreement at work, then you may have a *coordinate point lucid dream* on the astral, where you are performing a symbolically related action. The action in the lucid dream may not have anything to do with negotiating business agreements. It might, for example, have you trying to hoist a boat up onto a trailer. Yet the process of you mentally working through hoisting the boat up onto the trailer in the dream has coordinate point significance for your real world attempt to negotiate the agreement at work.

This doesn't mean that if you can't hoist the boat in your dream, that you won't be able to negotiate the agreement in physical life. It is more of a sandbox or test-bed situation, where your psyche can safely begin working on a problem in a lucid dream environment. This allows for the scaffolding of thoughts, testing of intentions and the seeking of further information about what may be required.

All this is taking place in an environment that is not going to panic the conscious ego because the boat or trailer hoist doesn't contain the actual items associated with the stressful negotiated business agreement that is being contemplated in the physical world. In other circumstances, when the conscious ego feels less threatened in deliberating over a physical act, the reference dreams can more closely mirror the actual situation that is desired. Then you may find yourself lucid dreaming about closing a deal or negotiation that you wish to complete in physical reality.

Astral Telekinesis 2
Monday 13 July 2015 – Lucid Flying Dream

I'm looking at a large sailboat in dock and then decide to jump behind the wheel. There was some concern about whether I would damage the sailboat in the process of sailing it out into the open water, but it was unharmed. Now clear of the dock, I was able to lift this big sailboat, plus all the men crewing it, into the air with my own thought-force.

I "sailed" the boat above the treetops for a distance until we reached the area we were looking for. Carefully and safely, I brought the boat down undamaged. We disembarked and moved through the forest to meet up with the people we were seeking.

Flight Notes:

Many present disciplines of science such as psychology and neurology, mostly view us as individuals who are mentally and emotionally cut off from each other. Yes, we can share conversation during the day, but these disciplines would say that what happens when we go to bed and dream each night only happens in our own heads and that there are no "connections" possible between people. I will have more to say about such connections in our next book.

Molecular Experiment 1
Tuesday 15 November 2016 – Lucid Flying Dream

I was near a building and decided to fly over it. I started to take off as usual and noticed a weak gravity really close to the earth. The higher I travelled, the less control I seemed to have. Once I reached a certain height, gravity seemed to be working in reverse making it easier to keep going up than back down. There was also an astral current drifting me in a definite direction. The current did not feel like an earth-based wind, that is variable in pressure. Instead, it felt more like a constant current which worked steadily on me, creating resistance if I dared go against it.

I was of a mind to try some experiments. First, I tried simple thought-power to move myself in a direction against the current. On this occasion I was unsuccessful, as my thought force was not strong enough to counteract it. Then I came up with a new idea that unfolded something like this:

Instead of pushing myself against the current, perhaps I can change the structure of the current itself by using my own thought force and visualization?

I then used my thoughts to create an anchor point at the origin position of the drift. Next, I made a mental path between the origin point and my position. Following this, I had a deliberate and strong thought to change the structure of the molecules in the astral current between me and the origin point, so that they would cease to push against me in the same way.

On the execution of this thought there was a shudder and halt to my drift for a few seconds. It felt like I had discovered something, but then the current picked straight back up and I recommenced drifting again under its influence. I was left wondering what sort of thought-force would have been required to neutralize the impact of the current on me for any length of time?

Flight Notes:

In the physical world when it comes to matter, we are usually working with it in a macro-context, with the object as a whole. The really exciting thing about astral environments is that we are not restricted to the macro-scale and can conduct matter experiments at the molecular level by just using our thoughts. Such experiments can have fascinating results and open us up to new ways of thinking. It is worth repeating here that such abilities are not superpowers and are part of the everyday inner heritage that we all have access to as human beings. As you read in the dream description I could only muster the requisite thought force to pause the impact of the astral current for a few seconds. I feel strongly that the efforts of one person could be enhanced by the addition of others perhaps through a combined meditation or trance state. Providing a combined thought force that could be directed into some fascinating areas of experimentation in physics and astronomy.

I also feel that such *combined consciousness* experiments could lead to healing opportunities that add to our present practice in physical medicine.

[Pain Management Test]

Disclaimer: The following is a visualization exercise for you to test your ability to manage a mild pain experience and is not designed as an alternative to pain medication or clinical treatment. If you are suffering from a mild, substantial or mysterious pain you should visit your doctor or clinician as soon as possible.

The exercise: Next time you are not feeling well visualize the molecules and atoms that make up the etheric or astral version of the organ or part of your body that is the source of the pain.

Visualize it as being out of balance in ways that correspond to your discomfort. You could imagine that the electrons are spinning the wrong way or that the atoms and molecules are not combining in the right structures. Now using your own mental and emotional thought force, visualize the electrons slowing down and changing spin to the correct way. Visualize the break-up of the problem atoms and molecules and gradually replace them with healthy ones.

Visualize the corrected patterns of consciousness and energy flowing through from the astral and etheric versions of the organ to the physical organ or body part that was experiencing the pain.

How did you go? Did this exercise provide you with any relief to your mild pain experience?

Molecular Experiment 2
Thursday, 19 January 2017 - Lucid Dream

I was looking at a brick wall and then through the manipulation of my mind I was able to change the molecules of the bricks, so the wall was no longer there.

Flight Notes:

Whilst this might sound like a demonstration from a Hollywood film like "Dr. Strange", the ability to rearrange objects on the astral is something any of us can do. Nonetheless, it does require you to believe that you can do it. If you don't believe it is possible, then you are unlikely to form the necessary thought structures to make it happen. This can be an easy thing to say, but not so much an easy thing to do, as most of us bring our earth-bound ideas of limitation into the lucid dream world. Or in other words, "I can't do X on Earth so surely I can't do X whilst I'm lucid-dreaming." Whether it's rearranging matter or flying across the sky in the astral you need to find a way to give yourself permission.

Lucid Participation
Monday, 27 February 2017 - Lucid Flying Dream

I began to fly in an astral current that was moving in the same direction as my flight. This assisted me to fly from my house to another house at high speed. On a second flight in the same direction, I decided to add a little thought-force of my own which increased my speed temporarily, and then my velocity dropped back to the speed of the current.

Flight Notes:

There is a creative tension in lucid-dreaming. Sometimes the dream wants to take you in a certain direction and the smartest thing is just to go with the flow. The benefit of doing this is that it doesn't require you to make as many active changes to your participation, which is more economical with your conscious resources. Making it less likely you'll bump out of the dream. You are still lucid and experiencing the dream to its fullest effect, you're just not pushing up against the events, trying to radically change the outcome. Some lucid dreamers place a high value on being able to have maximum influence on the course of a lucid dream. Occasionally lucid dream environments will allow for this, but more often a fine balance is required between participating, directing and choosing action.

Double Projection
Friday, 11 August 2017 – Lucid Flying Dream

I found myself in a cold city park bounded by a major road and I had materialized into a standing position at the top of some steps. Looking ahead out onto the scene in front of me, I immediately had the desire to fly forwards up into the air. But on this occasion, it was not an automatic process, as I had not projected my consciousness into the appropriate subtle body necessary for flight. I then proceeded to raise two of my fingers in front of my face to help with concentration and pushed out the required subtle body. The process of leaving my present dream-body for the newer "flyable" one was very pleasurable in an electrical sense.

Flight Notes:

I have no doubt that some lucid dreams can provide you with the opportunity to experience real physical places. I have found two main ways to do this. First, one can visit a place via an out-of-body experience. Or secondly, one can emotionally magnetize features from the desired place back towards oneself via an expansion of consciousness.

If you are interested to try either of these, here are some pointers that I have picked up along the way.

- Mentally set the intention of where you would like to visit before you go to sleep.
- Cultivate patience. This is not like dialling for pizza and could require repetition over many nights, weeks or months before progress is made.
- Touch, meaningfully hold and meditate on a physical item that relates to the place that you want information about before bed.
- Research the place you are hoping to link with. The more focused the study, the easier it should be to make progress.

Astral Etiquette

If you try to intentionally astrally link with another person using lucid dreaming <u>do not assume</u> you will be granted information they do not want to give. In my experience, there seems to be some sort of permissions system at play that makes it difficult to be sensitive to information from people who do not want to give it at their heart level. Having etiquette for the privacy of others and being sensitive to their needs seems to be a prerequisite for being granted some level of access. The most powerful tool that you can bring into play here is your own empathy and compassion for the suffering of others.

Timber Log
Sunday, 3 June 2018 - Lucid Flying Dream

I had a lucid-flying dream where I flew over the mouth of Botany Bay, south of Sydney. There were massive waves and strong currents below me as I flew across the wide watery expanse. I made it to the other side where there was a shipping fuel depot. I was able to straddle a large timber log with my legs and then had the idea to lift both myself and the log into the air, like a man riding a tree trunk. I was able to do all of this with my own mind, which was a milestone for my lucid dreaming ability.

Flight Notes:

It was another dream where it felt like I was out of my body and visiting a real physical place. I do not believe that I lifted a real physical log during this experience but rather the astral counterpart or equivalent of such a log that may have been lying around.

Mass increase
Sunday, 11 August 2019 - Lucid Flying Dream

I was travelling past a number of very beautiful destinations with crystal clear water. The sheer beauty of the places roused my critical facility and desire to store the environments to memory so I might return to them at some future point.

I decided to gradually rise into the air at the edge of a river reaching the highest point over clear water and then gradually made my way down. As I landed on the other side of the river, I felt my mass increase as I made contact with the ground and sank into the green grass.

Flight Notes:

As my feet sank into the ground, the feeling of my mass increasing was visceral and palpable. Intuitively I found myself wondering why I would experience a feeling of substantially increasing mass on contact with the ground? I feel it could have something to do with the one meter ground level gravity layer described in some of my previous lucid dreams.

Projection into Matter
Tuesday 2 July 2019 - Lucid Dream

At first it seemed like I had projected into a boat that was being tossed around at sea. There was a woman talking on the boat and I could hear her voice, but the clarity was about 60-65%. It was going to take a massive extra effort to be able to hear her clearly and I couldn't summon that extra focus to make it happen in the lucid dream. The most startling thing about this dream was not so much that I was in the boat, but rather that I had projected into the wood that the boat hull was made of. Or in other words, into the structure of the boat as opposed to being inside the boat as a passenger.

The feeling of "being the boat hull" rolling with the bump and toss of the waves was kinetically palpable and I was aware of sensations coming strongly through to my physical body on the bed, which felt like it was being tossed and turned, even though I was still lying face down in a fixed position. The dream then shifted into another environment and again I found myself projecting into physical matter - in this case a four-wheel drive car.

I had not projected to the passenger seat but was instead sandwiched somewhere under the driver's seat and above the gearbox. I could clearly hear a voice, but couldn't see the driver and passenger from where I was, apart from the odd flash of an arm moving the gear stick.

The sensation of being squashed by the bodyweight of the driver as the car undulated up and down over rough four-wheel drive terrain was extraordinary. Feeling the crunch and bob of the gear stick changing gears, as though it was going right through me was weird, all the while listening to the driver talking to the passenger. In this case, the audio clarity was about 50%.

I could barely understand the conversation. It was like hearing someone talking in the next room. Again, there was just so much to deal with physically - coping with all the sensations flowing back to my physical body on the bed - that I couldn't spare the conscious resources to concentrate enough on what was being said.

While this lucid dream "car projection" was happening, my body in bed was lying stomach-down, with my face on the pillow. Above me there was some type of strange and strong vertical force pinning me down to the bed through the back of my heart chakra. I felt like a crab being fixed to the bed by a shaft of magnetized light. Despite this, there was no pain, just a feeling of being squashed through my back and being pinned down onto the bed.

I was then out of the car dream and into a chemical build-up process for a large release of lucid dream-flying fuel. I recognized all the signs and played my part, but my lucidity was too high and I found myself too awake to keep a hold on the dream. It was like I had been given the opportunity to fly a jet but I couldn't stay in the cockpit. So I just lay there on my bed, fully awake with all the mysterious residual down-force still pressing into my back's heart chakra.

I slowly began to resist it and then finally turned over in my bed to spend some minutes making sure that I fixed all of the dream details to my conscious memory before I allowed myself to fall back asleep.

Flight notes:

I have had other lucid dreams where I have moved through matter, but never like this had I projected directly into and remained in solid matter before. It was a new experience.

Lucid Flying Dreams Summary

This brings us to the end of our lucid dreams in this book. We hope that you have enjoyed the journey. Some of you will hopefully by now be motivated to expand your own lucid dreaming experiences?

8. Lucid Checklist

Here are some handy ideas to help improve your potential to lucid dream.

Trauma

If you are at a stage of your life that involves a lot of trauma related to family, work, health or other things, then it's usually going to be more difficult to remember your dreams during this time. You could feel so stressed out just coping with life that you can't spare the "mental bandwidth" to try and lucid dream.

Rather than feel worried about this or stressing yourself further, I suggest that you "park" your desire to lucid dream and make peace with your present circumstances, as unpleasant as they may be and work through them inch by inch. Eventually your inbuilt resilience should deliver you through such trauma to a calmer place where you can resume your "parked" desire to lucid dream.

Calm Tips

If you are finding that it's taking too long to reach a state of calm and you would like some assistance, here are some visualizations to help.

Firstly, most of our stress is linked to our physical body consciousness and an idea that we are a body, trapped in time and circumstance. We can progress by unhooking from this idea and instead visualizing our fundamental nature as being an indestructible travelling lucid consciousness (astral body) that just happens to use the physical body as day-time house or place of residence.

Second, we are going to ask you to visualize that this fundamental travelling consciousness is capable of surviving every disaster possible including the loss of your job, your family, your partner, your health, all of your income and assets and even the death of your physical body.

Third, visualize and meditate on this idea of indestructibility, that you are more than your physical body and that you will survive anything and everything that life can throw at you. If you can do this successfully you will be creating some space between your physical body and your inner consciousness. Thinking, feeling and talking yourself into this space will give rise to a state of calm that helps with lucid dreaming.

How do you know if you've found the space?

Life should seem less like something that is happening to you and more like something you are watching and participating in with a curious and heartfelt intention.

Getting Comfortable

If you had no trouble with the visualization of yourself as a travelling, lucid consciousness then it's no wonder that many of us feel uncomfortable in the physical body that is comparatively thicker, heavier and lacking in as much mobility.

Most people I speak with report they feel happiest when they have a sensation of lightness and freedom. But how do we make that happen when we are feeling flat, dense and run down?

I find the simplest way to get comfortable with our physical body is to stop thinking about where we should be *dragging* our body, or what we should be *doing* with it and instead embark on the science of how to be very comfortable in our body when it's doing nothing.

Unfortunately if left to its own devices, the physical body will dehydrate, eat sugary food, seek artificial stimulants, avoid exercise and generally roll up into a tight and weak, inflexible mass of unhappiness.

If you are over-invested in your physical body consciousness, you could encounter problems with any of the following: sugar, sex addiction, alcohol, weight, caffeine, fitness, flexibility, inflammation, sleep and anxiety. The body is calling the shots and the rest of you is going along for the ride.

If we desire to have ample reserves of will power for lucid dreaming advancement, then we need to recall power over the body away from the physical body consciousness and give it back to our mind as the rightful governor of the body.

In advanced lucid dreaming, the mind is using its will to bend and move the etheric or astral body in question to suit its own purposes. Accordingly, having a strong will with good mental and emotional control bodes well for lucid dreaming. Ironically, the best tool we have handy to develop and grow these abilities is our physical body.

Success requires us to be scientific about this. Which food and drinks generate calm in you for the longest period of time? What is your favorite exercise before relaxing? What is the perfect time to go to bed? Who are your most easy going friends? What is your perfect shower or bath routine? What are the best shows to watch that make you feel clear and focused? What are the most inspiring books you like to read? What activities do you participate in that raise your consciousness?

Heart Listening

Are you head-focused or heart-focused? Many of us at work are living in a head-focused world that prioritizes thinking over feeling. It can be too easy to for us to roll along and forget we actually are here on Earth to help others as opposed to serving ourselves. If we can make some extra time to simply *listen* to someone who is having issues or problems then it can also make a big difference to our lucid dreaming experience. Moreover you don't have to be an expert counsellor to hear someone's problems. You don't even need to offer any advice. The important thing is to be actively and genuinely listening to them with all your heart that will, by itself, make a difference to the person's suffering.

Do this heart listening successfully and then by some force of reciprocity you may be returned some enhanced lucid dreaming experiences. By the way, if after listening you feel that your friend's issues are serious then you could consider recommending the services of a qualified clinician with therapeutic skills to assist them.

Affinity Networks

If you can develop an affinity with certain causes or programs that have good intentions, (i.e. a sports club, chess group, community action, beach cleanup, dog lovers, environment, plant lovers, student mentoring, volunteer fire fighting, aged care, community services etc) then such networks will put you into affinity with certain people and provide opportunities for you to meet and talk with them.

I need to emphasize that this has to involve interaction with real people. It is not enough for you to join an online group, read a few articles and expect to see changes in your lucid dreaming outcomes. Affinity networks require genuine, heartfelt human connections *en rapport* that create their own energy to drive certain types of lucid dreaming activity. The most common affinity networks are ones that we develop inside of our workplaces around certain social issues and challenges.

Rise

If you wish to take your lucid dreaming to the next level, I suggest conducting a life audit. As you have seen from my own lucid truth, lucid dreaming sometimes requires you to be able to "see" things that are further away. This is unlikely to occur unless we have found a way to rise a little higher.

The simplest visualization that I can give for this is to imagine yourself flying through the air. Now consider all your regular behaviors and habits and decide which ones contribute to you flying higher and also all those that pull you down? This doesn't mean that we should walk out on our responsibilities as successfully dealing with obstacles and challenges can raise us higher. If you are having difficulty classifying your activities and habits into "low" and "high" then I can hint that the biggest boosts I have received to my lucid dreaming "far-sightedness" are related to work-based milestones associated with the helping others.

Critical Facility

> "Curiosity. Go after your curiosity." Ada Yonath, Nobel Prize Winner in Chemistry

When dreaming, don't expect to remember everything all the time, as some dreams are not important for the conscious ego to experience directly. The process of entering into lucidity seems to go something like this for me. I am participating in a dream activity that is going on for some time beneath my conscious awareness but somehow I have been able to retain a little bug or listening/watching device over it. This little bug or critical facility sits patiently watching, waiting and experiencing until the dream drama introduces vision, characters, scenery or events that rouse my critical facility into a higher level of action. I am then brought into a state of greater lucidity, awareness, participation and memory recording in the dream that becomes "lucid". My lucid dream entry point usually appears sometime after the actual beginning of the wider dream and only when events become interesting to me.

Consequently, cultivating your curiosity is key to developing your critical facility. How does one do this? You could take the conventional route and read widely, participate in events & engage in debate and discussion. It's also important to value your own *thinking* about things as an end in itself instead of worrying about having to produce something physical all the time. Trust yourself and if you are sometimes near children you can progress by kindly observing toddlers and babies who are wired to wonder.

We hope that our checklist section has provided you with some appropriate visualizations and tips to increase your lucid dreaming.

9. The hard problem of consciousness

What would our data set of lucid dreams have to say about the hard problem of consciousness posed below by David Chalmers:

> "How can we explain what it is like to entertain a mental image, or to experience an emotion? It is widely agreed that experience arises from a physical basis, but we have no good explanation of why and how it so arises. Why should physical processing give rise to a rich inner life at all? It seems objectively unreasonable that it should, and yet it does (Chalmers 1995)."

Creative Science would acknowledge that Mr. Chalmers has grounded his question in a foundational assumption, which states that such experiences, mental images, emotions and the like arise as a consequence of physical processing. Likewise, as lucid dreamers we are not able to escape the idea that consciousness, in a lucid-dreaming context, does require a functioning physical body. We are alive, sleeping on the bed while our lucid consciousness may be dream-flying or actively remembering our dreams. Both processes seem to require brain activity and also other parts of the body to support the process.

A conflict of sorts

This delivers us into a conflict of sorts. In the previous section, Lucid Checklist (Calm Tips), we provided you with a visualization that was based on the idea that a fundamental unit of your identity is a travelling lucid consciousness that is independent of and survives the physical body. Yet here in this section, we are saying that a travelling lucid consciousness must by definition require a living, organic, physical body to support it. So does a travelling lucid consciousness require a physical body to support it or not?

Our Next Book

In our next book *Creative Science and Visualization* we will deal with this question and also delve more deeply into exploring whether animals and plants experience consciousness? We will introduce more of our Creative Science Framework and deliver to you more lucid dreams that will stimulate your scientific curiosity and also push the limits of oddness. I personally invite you to join us for our next lucid dream rollercoaster ride as we help raise awareness about the wonderful diversity of accessible consciousness that surrounds us.

10.0 Glossary

Action potential: The probability of event or action occurring as a direct result of its stored electrical energy.

Anomalies: Odd things that don't make sense and are out of keeping with what is expected.

Amygdala: A key brain organ involved in lucid dreaming and consciousness that regulates and records the emotional intensity of experiences as they happen.

Astral: Extremely fine electromagnetic material.

Astral plane: A gateway universe that links a variety of physical and non-physical universes.

Astral body: A mobile, subtle and living counterpart of our physical body that is concerned with thoughts and the expression of emotions.

Astral current: A constant current of flow in a certain direction in the astral plane that causes resistance if you try to move against it.

Bellows breath: A type of breathing technique that can assist lucid consciousness to travel great distances.

Block universe: A theory of consciousness that allows for past, present and future to be all part of the same coincident point (or block) in space-time.

Bump out: Losing hold on the dream state due to a degree of lucidity that is too high.

Chakra: Energy portals that connect certain regions of the physical and subtle bodies.

Coordinate point lucid dream: A lucid dream "sandbox" or framework where the individual can attempt to work with ideas that relate to the achievement of an intended or contemplated action in the physical world.

Copenhagen Interpretation: Mathematical appendices that are designed to explain the difference between the quantum and macro-physical worlds.

Counterpart: The reflection or part of an object that is present and visible in another plane.

Creative Science: rational, methodical and organized investigation of the world beneath matter using lucid dreaming, meditation, trance and other non-drug induced states that support mobile human consciousness.

Creative tension: a timeline that sits between two points of opposing polarity, action, or effect.

Criterion method: A way of increasing lucidity during a dream by the continuous rational investigation of the dream environment.

Critical facility: An analytical mode of consciousness that allows us to process, think about and classify events as they happen.

CSF: Cerebrospinal fluid or clear liquid that the brain floats in and which circulates throughout the spinal column.

Dark matter: A theory about the world beneath matter that it is made up of dark matter that cannot be observed.

Dementia: A condition of altered consciousness where the continuity of memory recall may be broken into uneven intervals that may or may not hold data that the individual is able to effectively communicate.

Dream body: see subtle body

Electron: A very small negatively charged, spinning mobile particle that orbits around the nucleus of an atom.

Entanglement: Two particles are said to be entangled with each other if a change in the phase of one particle causes a coincident change in the phase of the other (entangled) particle.

Ether: Extremely fine viscous, liquid electromagnetic layer that lies between the physical and astral worlds.

Etheric body: A subtle body that is closely aligned with our physical body and responsible for supporting organ function by delivering energy from outside of the body to the organs.

Etheric plane: A universe that contains etheric counterparts to every item of physical matter.

Etiquette: A mode of behavior that allows for the appropriate consideration of others.

Friction: Resistance caused when two objects in contact inhibit each other's movement and motion.

Glide flying: An exhilarating lucid dream slow motion style glide-walk above and within one meter of the ground surface.

Go with the flow: A lucid dreaming strategy that involves a low level of participatory intervention by the lucid dreamer in the sequence of dream events.

Grand Unified Theory: A theory that is able to join up the four forces of light, gravity, nuclear and electromagnetic forces into a single explainable event horizon. Our expanded GUT definition in this book also includes the experience of consciousness, the world beneath matter and the limits of time and space.

Hippocampus: A key brain organ involved with lucid dreaming and consciousness that helps us to remember the content matter and sequence of events.

In dual: A hybrid state of consciousness where one can be aware of two different bodies at the same time. For example, you could be aware of your physical body on the bed and also your dreaming consciousness (astral body) at the same time.

Inner heritage: The inner world that each of us has available to us as a part of being human.

Inertia: Is the resistance of any physical object to a change in its velocity.

Integrated Information Theory: A theory of consciousness that says consciousness arrives or appears from a constant stream of thoughts.

Interpenetration: An event where more than one object is able to take up the same place in physical space at the same time.

Lucid: An alert state of consciousness where one is able to accurately remember and recall events.

Lucid dream: A dream where the dreamer is able to clearly remember the details of the dream experience and their participatory role in it.

Lucid dreaming: Training the conscious mind to participate in the dreaming process by making decisions and remembering the minutiae of dream details for later recording.

Lucid dream flying fuel: An indeterminate mixture of available brain hormones, proteins in the blood and mineral by products left over from in-brain chemical processes that support some types of out of body experiences.

Lucid truth: The personal, unassailable truth of your direct lucid experience carefully and honestly recorded for the benefit of yourself and others.

Many Worlds: The Many Worlds theory of quantum mechanics is based on the work of physicist Hugh Everett who provided a universal wave function mathematical proof that is able to join the quantum and physical worlds together as part of one system.

Measurement problem: A problem that emerges in quantum physics when the mathematically predicted position of a particle differs from the measured position, such that the act of measurement interferes with the probable location of the particle.

Molecule: A grouping of atoms that is a building block of physical matter.

Multiverse: A description given to the infinite number of parallel worlds associated with the Many Worlds theory of quantum mechanics.

Odd: A characteristic of an object or event that is not in keeping with our expectations.

Out-of-body experience: A remembered mobilization of consciousness outside of the physical body during lucid dreaming, meditation, trance or other states of mindfulness.

Panpsychism: A theory that allows for a diversity of consciousness in humans, plants, animals and also inanimate matter, such as rocks.

Plane: A distinct dimension or universe with its own native physics that allows for the expression of some form of consciousness.

Personality: The ego or daily conscious operator of the mind/body.

Probable realities: Parallel worlds that provide for the full expression of human experience including all decisions taken and not taken.

Probable future: A possible future for you or someone else that already exists in a parallel world.

Probable past: One of yours, or someone else's, past experiences on a parallel or probable world.

Probable self: Another version of you or someone else that exists on a parallel or probable world.

Psyche: A grouping that includes the ego and the subconscious.

Signature: Observeable material that suggests the presence or former presence of an object or event.

String Theory: A theory about the world beneath matter that it is made up of tiny strings that stretch throughout the universe as the building blocks of matter.

Subtle bodies: Extremely fine electromagnetic counterparts of the physical body that play a role in the equalization and inner balancing of a person.

Quantum mechanics: The study of extremely small particles such as electrons and photons.

Telekinesis: Movement of objects in the astral plane using thought power.

Trajectory: The path of an object in motion.

Viscous: Describing the relative thickness of a liquid that creates resistance as you move through it.

References

Definition of "Odd" in the Cambridge Dictionary <https://dictionary.cambridge.org/dictionary/english/odd>.

Crull, E (2019), If you thought Quantum Mechanics was weird you need to check out Entangled Time, Physics in Science Alert.

Funk, C (2018), Daubert Versus Frye: A National Look at Expert Evidentiary Standards, The Expert Institute, <https://www.theexpertinstitute.com>.

Barrett, A (2018), Why we need to figure out a theory of consciousness, The Conversation.

Byrne (2008), The Many Worlds of Hugh Everett, Scientific American.

Somerville M (1846) Introduction, On the Connections of the Physical Sciences, Harper Brothers, New York.

Francis (2016) A GUT feeling about physics: Scientists want to connect the fundamental forces of nature in one Grand Unified Theory. Symmetry Magazine, <https://www.symmetrymagazine.org/article/a-gut-feeling-about-physics>.

The Physics arXiv Blog (2014) Why Physicists Are Saying Consciousness Is A State Of Matter, Like a Solid, A Liquid Or a Gas, <https://medium.com/the-physics-arxiv-blog/why-physicists-are-saying-consciousness-is-a-state-of-matter-like-a-solid-a-liquid-or-a-gas-5e7ed624986d>.

Heaven, D (2015) The human universe: Does consciousness create reality?, Space, New Scientist.

Keller (1984) A Feeling for the Organism: The Life and Work of Barbara McClintock.

Phelps (2006) Emotion and Cognition: Insights from Studies of the Human Amygdala, Annu. Rev. Psychol.

Siegel (2016) What every layperson should know about String Theory, Forbes, Science Contributor Group, <https://www.forbes.com/sites/startswithabang/2016/11/25/what-every-layperson-should-know-about-string-theory/#6e7916765a53>.

Tate (2013) Dark Matter and Dark Energy: The Mystery Explained, (Infographic), <https://www.space.com/20502-dark-matter-universe-mystery-infographic.html>.

McGaugh, Cahill, Roozendahl (1996) Involvement of the amygdala in memory storage: Interaction with other brain systems, Proc. Natl. Acad. Sci. USA Vol. 93, pp. 13508–13514, Colloquium Paper.

Low, (2012) The Cambridge Declaration on Consciousness Cambridge University.

Sample, I (2018) Stephen Hawking's final theory sheds light on the multiverse, The Guardian.

Sample, I (2019) Group of biologists tries to bury the idea that plants are conscious, The Guardian, <https://www.theguardian.com/science/2019/jul/03/group-of-biologists-tries-to-bury-the-idea-that-plants-are-conscious>.

Navilon (2019) The past, present and future exist simultaneously: The block universe theory, Ideapod <https://ideapod.com/the-past-present-and-future-exist-simultaneously-controversial-new-theory/>.

Dizikes (2015) Does time pass? Philosopher Brad Skow's new book says it does — but not in the way you may think, <https://news.mit.edu/2015/book-brad-skow-does-time-pass-0128>.

Sanz, Zamberlan, Erowid, Erowid, Tagliazucchi (2018) The Experience Elicited by Hallucinogens Presents the Highest Similarity to Dreaming within a Large Database of Psychoactive Substance Reports, Frontiers in Neuroscience, 12: 7.

Roberts J (1970) Session 741 A Seth Book: The Unknown Reality, Vol 2.

Grant (2019) Winged Pharaoh, Blackstone Audio, first published in 1937.

Chalmers, D (1995) Facing up to the problem of consciousness, Journal of Consciousness Studies, 2 (3): 200–219.

University of Cambridge (2019) How many solar systems are there?, 2009 - 2019 Institute of Astronomy, University of Cambridge https://www.ast.cam.ac.uk/public/ask/2360

Nobel (2019) All Nobel Prizes in Physics
https://www.nobelprize.org/prizes/lists/all-nobel-prizes-in-physics

Damian Amamoo, Sydney, 2020